Stock Ma:

Day Trading

Property Investing

Passive Income

The 4 in 1 Investment Guide: How to Analyse Opportunities, Trade Stocks, Generate Passive Income and Reach Financial Freedom How to analyze opportunities, Trade Stocks, Generate Passive Income and Reach Financial Freedom.

William K. Bradford

Table of Contents

About the Author

For the past seven years, William K. Bradford has been heavily involved in the stock market and has become something of a wizard when it comes to investing in stocks. He is highly experienced when it comes to analyzing the market, choosing the best stocks to invest in, and determining when it's time to sell. He has counseled many investors about the ins and outs of the stock market and has helped both beginners and experts alike achieve financial success with his expert advice.

After years of counseling fellow investors, and receiving nothing but positive feedback, William K. Bradford finally decided to sit down and write the book that you have in your hands right now. *Stock Market | Day Trading | Property Investing | Passive Income* contains the culmination of seven years of professional stock market experience. Each tip, trick, method, and strategy are proven by William K. Bradford himself to be highly effective, and numerous professional investors stand by many of these strategies and plans.

Each strategy contained within this book has been developed to be as effective as possible, with maximum profits and minimal losses, so that you pocket as much cash as possible. However, it's very rare that someone becomes a millionaire overnight through the stock market. You'll need to be dedicated, motivated, and hard-working. Nothing good in life comes easy, and you'll have to be determined if you want to find success in this industry.

William K. Bradford has full confidence in the contents of this book, and he is absolutely certain that if you use *Stock Market | Day Trading | Property Investing | Passive Income* correctly, your financial dreams will come true.

Stock Market

Chapter One:

So You Want to Invest in Stocks

The Stock Market is but one of the many possible ways you could choose to invest your hard-earned money. So why choose stocks rather than the other possibilities, like property or antiques?

To put it simply, the main reason that clever investors decide to invest in the stock market is because it provides the greatest potential returns. Also, when thinking about the long-term, there is no other kind of investment that performs as well and as consistently as the stock market.

The main drawback is the volatile nature of the market. The value of stocks can plummet during the short-term and can sometimes even drop for a protracted period. Bad timing or just plain bad luck can tank your returns in an instant, but the risk of this can be reduced significantly by opting to take a more long-term approach to investing.

There is no guarantee that you're going to see any kind of positive return. And, if you are unfortunate enough to pick stocks that depreciate in value consistently, you might even lose money in the long-term. But that's what draws most people to the stock market, isn't it? High risk, high reward.

Thankfully, you have in your hands one of the best tools a prospective stock market investor can own. By using this guide to educate yourself about the ins and outs of this market, you can make the risk more than acceptable for the expected reward. I will be showing you how to pick the right businesses and stocks to own, and which ones you should avoid.

Over the long term, putting in the extra effort is so worth it, since your money is able to work harder for you in equities than it would in pretty much any other investment. As you might already know, it is quite impossible to predict how the stock market is going to shift and change.

Yet, even with this unpredictability, the benefits that investing in stocks hold remain as multitudinous as ever. What has changed, or might still need to change, is the perception that the investor has of the stock market and the risks that it is associated with. Let's consider some of the reasons that stocks remain one of the best investments, and why you should invest in the market, regardless of your caliber.

Starting cheap

There's no reason that you have to give up thousands of dollars to dip your toes into the stock market. Stock investment is a commonly tread path to making money go further, and you can start by setting aside the couple of dollars you would usually spend to buy a coffee, and investing the total at the end of the month in stocks.

This is a pretty much painless way to use your earnings towards your future. As a novice investor with only a little bit of disposable income, a great way to begin is to place your money in an index fund. You could also push your luck with a DRIP, or a dividend reinvestment plan, which is offered by a wide variety of major companies. They do not require much experience, effort, or money.

Once you are in possession of at least one share, or a fractional share, of stock in a company that provides DRIP, you will be able to sign up for the DRIP and avoid needing to pay broker commissions. This is done by purchasing additional shares straight from the company or the company's agent. Any dividends that your stock earns will be reinvested automatically into more shares, or more fractional shares. Ideally, these should earn dividends of their own.

Essentially, what this means is that over a period of a few years, your stock earnings and holdings will be able to **compound,** or grow, at an accelerating rate without you needing to fork out more money or keep tabs on your investment.

Increase Your Wealth

It's vital that you understand that, if you do decide to invest in the stock market, there is no guarantee as to how your stocks are going to perform. The market is volatile, so you will need to be prepared for anything. Still, you don't need to buy stocks in the next Apple or Microsoft to earn a decent return.

Think about this: the stock market has averaged an annual return on investments of about ten percent since 1926, as measured by the S&P 500. This is despite the volatility of the market and its tendency to change at a rapid pace, sometimes resulting in a devastating crash, which is characterized by a sudden decline ranging in the double-digits.

However, volatile the market may be, there is no denying that there is some great money to be made from investing in stocks. If you are willing to take the necessary risks and have comes to terms with the fact that you may lose some money from time to time, then the stock market can make you rich.

Avoid Inflation

When you are trying to save your money for a major outlay, such as financing a good retirement or purchasing a home, inflation can be your worst enemy. Consider the fact that the inflation rate in the United States historically hovers around three percent. This could dig into the purchasing ability of money that is sitting in a CD, also known as a certificate of deposit, or a savings account.

Your money would need to earn at least three percent in order to keep up with the rate of inflation, and even savings accounts with high yields do not offer much more than two percent. You are generally able to earn a higher interest rate on certificates of deposit than you can on savings accounts, and you may even be capable of surpassing the inflation rate, if not merely keep up with it.

The drawback is that your money is tied up for the period of the CD, which can range anywhere from 30 days to 10 years. If you are in a situation where you would need to withdraw the money before the period ends, you will have to face an early withdrawal penalty, which will decrease your earnings further.

Know That the Stock Market is Not Working Against You

The stock market has no regard for your plans and where you want them to take you. It does not have an agenda, nor is it capable of having one, and it does not care about yours - not even a little bit. Despite what you think you know, based on spam emails and late-night infomercials, there are no magical formulas that will guarantee your investing success.

There are no secret handshakes, gestures, or passwords, and the rich and famous are not hiding any secrets that made them rich. There is very little between you and being a successful investor, other than a good understanding of the basics of investing and a little bit of research. You'll need to know how to apply the 'buy low, sell high' principal, and how the prices of stocks are determined.

Once you are familiar with the basics of stock market investing (which this guide will help you understand), then you will be well on your way to becoming a successful investor.

Take Your Time

You do not need to go out right now and rush to invest in the stock market. In fact, doing so is the best way to ensure failure. Instead, take the time to read through this guide thoroughly, do your homework, set realistic goals and expectations for yourself, and determine how you are going to use the information in this guide to the best of your ability, and in a way that is advantageous to you.

There are a number of online tools available to helpyou practice your investment strategies and help you get a feel for the volatility of the market, without spending any of your real, hard-earned money. Also, keep in mind that, while the market can, at times, seem unforgiving, investing can be an extremely lucrative and interesting endeavor.

Of course, the best way to learn to swim is to jump into the deep end. If you have enough disposable income, and aren't afraid to take a risk, you could always dive straight into the market. This is not recommended, though, since you'll always have a better chance at success if you are educated and prepared.

You Don't Need to Be a Genius

Even though a more experienced investor might have an advantage over you when you are first getting started, you do not need to be rich or a brainiac mathematician to be able to invest in the stock market. The requirements for investing in the stock market are quite modest in comparison to creating your own business from scratch or investing in a franchise.

At most, you will need to regularly set aside some money each month to invest. Research the companies that you are considering investing in, like reading their annual reports that can be found on their websites, and understanding pretty basic math, like addition, subtraction, division, multiplication, and working with decimals and fractions.

Stock market investment is for anyone and everyone with the drive, determination, and motivation to persist and accept risks. If you're able to learn from each of your failures, which are inevitable in any industry, then you have already taken the first step to becoming a successful stock market investor.

The stock market can be seen as more of a tool to make your financial dreams a reality. What we've discussed in this chapter is merely the beginning of a field with much more depth, and the rest of this guide will help you understand all the details of the stock market. Try not to get overwhelmed! There's still a long way to go.

Chapter Two:
Classifying Stocks

There is a lot more involved in investing in the stock market than simply purchasing shares, or stock, in a company and calling it a day. There are a number of different classes of stocks, all of which can be classified into two types: Common Stock and Preferred Stock. In this chapter, I am going to discuss the different stock classes that fall into these two categories, and what it means to buy the different stock types.

Common Stock

As the name suggests, common stock is, simply put, common. This is the type of stock that most people are talking about when discussing stocks in general, and the majority of stock on the stock market is issued in the form of common stock. In essence, common shares represent ownership in a company, and a claim, or dividends, in a portion of its profits.

Investors are allowed one vote per share to elect members of the board, who will then oversee the major decisions that the management makes. When considering the long term, common stock yields much higher returns than pretty much all other investments, by means of capital growth. This higher return does, however, come at a cost, as the majority of common stocks come with the highest risk attached.

If a company goes bankrupt and is forced to liquidate, those who hold common shares will not receive any cash until the bondholders, creditors, and preferred shareholders are paid - hence the risk. This leads us to the second type of stock: preferred stock.

Preferred Stock

Like common stock, preferred stock is a representation of some degree of ownership of a company. However, unlike common stock, it does not come with the same rights for voting, though this may vary from company to company. Investors are generally guaranteed a fixed dividend forever with preferred shares. This differs from common stock in that common stock does not have any guaranteed dividends.

Another advantage to preferred stock is that, in the event of liquidation, shareholders with preferred stock are paid before those with common stocks, albeit still after debt holders. Preferred stock can also be callable, which means that the company can purchase the shares from its shareholders at a time of their choosing, for any reason, usually for a premium as well.

Many people consider preferred stock to be more of a debt than an equity. It helps to think of these shares as being in the place between common shares and bonds.

Other stock types

Industry

Companies are generally divided by industry, which are usually called sectors. Stocks that belong to the same sector, such as energy or technology sectors, might shift together in response to economic or market events. This is why it is so important to diversify your portfolio by investing in stocks across various sectors.

Company size

If you've done any research about the stock market, you may have heard the terms mid-cap or large-cap. These terms refer to the capitalization of the market, or how valuable a company is. Usually, companies are separated into three 'buckets' by size:

- **Large cap:** market value of $10 billion or more

- **Mid cap:** market value between $2 billion and $10 billion

- **Small cap:** market value between $300 million and $2 billion

Style

Sometimes, stocks are described as value or growth. Growth stocks are provided by companies that are either growing at a rapid pace, or are expected to grow quickly. Investors are usually willing to pay more for these kinds of stocks since they can expect greater returns.

On the other hand, value stocks are basically on sale. These are the stocks that have been deemed undervalued and underpriced by investors. It is assumed that these stocks are going to appreciate in value, as they are either suffering from a short-term event or going undetected.

Location

Stocks are also usually grouped by their geographical location. You are able to diversify your investment portfolio by investing in companies that do business internationally, as well as in emerging markets, which are market areas that are expected to experience some growth.

Now that we've covered the basic categories of stock, it's time to look at their various classifications and the implications that these classifications have.

Class of Shares/Stocks

In order to understand the different classes of stocks, it's important to understand what a class of shares actually is.

What is a class of share?

Essentially, a class of shares is a type of stock listed by a company that is differentiated by the level of voting rights received by the shareholders. For example, a company could have two classes of shares, or classes of stock, which we'll call Class A and Class B for the sake of simplicity. Company owners that have owned their company privately and choose to go public usually create Class A and Class B stock structures with different rights for voting.

This is done so that they can maintain control, and well as ensure that the company is not so easily targeted for a takeover. One of the most common of the stock classes is advisory shares, which are also called advisor shares. This stock type is given to business advisors in exchange for their expertise and insight.

The advisors that this type of stock option is offered to are founders of companies, or high-level executives. Usually, advisor shares invest monthly over a period of about two years, one a no-cliff schedule, and 100% trigger acceleration.

Understanding these classes

The term 'class of shares' can also refer to the various share classes that exist for numerous mutual funds. There are three different share classes: Class A, Class B, and Class C. These classes hold different sales charges, operating expenses, and 12b-1 fees. Whether referring to the multiple share classes that advisor-sold mutual funds offer, or the different classes of a company's stock, both of these cases refer to the different costs and rights owned by those who hold each share class. Simple, right?

Mutual fund share classes

Mutual funds sold by advisors can have different classes, each class having a fee structure and a unique sales charge. Class A mutual fund shares have lower 12b-1 fees, charge a front-end load and have operating expenses that are below average. Class B mutual fund shares have higher 12b-1 fees, charge a back-end load, and have higher operating expenses. Finally, Class C mutual fund shares do not have a front-end load, though back-end loads still apply, are considered level-load and have higher-than-average operating expenses.

Contingent deferred sales charge (CDSC), or the back-end load, can be eliminated or reduced, depending on the duration for which shares have been held. Class B shares will usually have a CDSC that is gone in as little as one year from the date they were purchased. Class C shares will generally start with a high CDSC, which will only completely disappear after about 5-10 years.

Chapter Three:
What's the Plan?

To be honest, buying stocks is not the difficult part. The challenge comes in when deciding which companies will benefit you - which are usually the companies that dominate the stock market consistently. This is where many prospective investors fall short and is why I've dedicated an entire chapter to choosing an investment plan.

The strategies that we're going to discuss in this chapter have been tried and tested countless times by numerous investors, and have been proven to work each time, without fail. Before I get started, here's one investment tip that could save your life: never invest more than 10% of your portfolio in individual stocks.

Don't Let Your Emotions Get
the Better of You

Being successful in the stock market has nothing to do with your intellect, as we've said before. Instead, you need to be able to fight and control the urges that tend to get other investors into trouble when buying and selling stocks. You need to be able to think both logically and emotionally about your investments and be able to make your decision based on your head and your gut.

Overthinking an investment can also lead to disaster. You need to think hard about your investments, but not so hard that you start to second guess everything, causing you to miss out on what could have been an incredible opportunity. Likewise, overactivity in trading led by your emotions is one of the easiest ways to hinder your returns on your portfolio.

Being able to balance your logic and your emotions will help you in the long run.

Choose Companies
Rather Than Ticker Symbols

It can be difficult to remember that behind the jumble of letters and numbers of stock quotes found drifting along the bottom of a news broadcast is an actual company owned by real people. Try not to let the stock market and buying stock become an abstract concept in your mind. Remember that when you buy a share of a company, you are becoming a part-owner of that business.

You are going to encounter some overwhelming information that might cause an overload when you are on the hunt for potential business partners. Think of it this way: it is far easier to track down the right company when you're wearing a hat that says, 'I buy businesses.' You want to see how a business operates, its competitors, its place in the industry as a whole, whether it brings something new to your portfolio, and its prospects in the long term.

Always Plan Ahead

All investors, at some point or another, face the temptation to alter their relationship status with their stocks. As I mentioned earlier, making decisions in the heat of the moment can lead to the infamous investment blunder of buying high and selling low. This is where strategizing, and journaling comes in handy.

Try to write down some of the things that make all of the stocks in your portfolio worth committing to, and while you have a clear head, the situations that would justify ending your relationship with some stocks. Why are you buying, and why are you selling?

Write down exactly what about a certain company is appealing to you, and what opportunities you see it presenting in the future. Determine what your expectations are, what metrics matter the most, and the milestones that you will judge the progress of the company by. Organize the pitfalls that might occur and take note of the ones that might change the game completely, and which ones would only be a temporary setback.

Likewise, there can be many good reasons to decide to cut off an investment. For this part of your planning process, try to develop an investment prenup that clearly states what would cause you to let go of a stock. Do not confuse this with the movement of stock prices, especially not in the short term.

Rather focus on the changes that are fundamental to the business, and that would influence the company's ability to grow over the long term. If the company suddenly loses a major customer, or a major competitor enters the market, or the successor of the CEO moves the business toward a different direction, or your investment plan does not pan out after some time.

These are all things that might prompt you to sell a stock, but they are not the only reasons. You may have different, more personal reasons for letting go of an investment, all of which should be written down in your journal or business plan.

Gradually Build Up Your Positions

Time is the superpower of the investor, not timing. All of the most prosperous investors in the world buy stocks because they expect a reward from them, whether it comes from dividends or price appreciation over a period of years or even decades. This means that you are able to take your time when buying as well. These are some strategies that can reduce your exposure to the volatility of price.

Buy in thirds

When you buy in thirds, you can avoid having your morale crushed by shaky results when you first start investing in the stock market. Divide the amount that you wish to invest by three, then pick three separate points to buy shares, as the name suggests. These could either be based on company events and performance, or at regular intervals.

To give an example, you may decide to purchase shares before a product is released, and then put the next third of your money into these shares if it turns out to be a success. If it turns out to be a failure, you could divert the rest of your money elsewhere.

Dollar-cost average

While this may sound like a complex concept, it is actually quite plain. Dollar-cost averaging involves investing a predetermined sum of money at regular intervals, like once a month or every few months. This amount is able to buy more shares when the price of the stock decreases, and fewer shares when its price increases.

Overall, it evens out the average price that you'll end up paying. There are even a few online brokerage firms that allow investors to set up investing schedules that are entirely automated.

Buy 'the basket'

If you are not able to decide which one company out of a group in a certain industry will be the winner in the long term, you could just buy them all! Buying a basket of stocks will remove the pressure of having to pick 'the one' that will be successful. Having stakes in all of the competitors that meet your expectations means that you will not miss out if one of them turns out to be a hit.

You will be able to use the earnings from the winner company to offset any losses from the others that were not as successful. You'll also be able to identify which company is 'the one', allowing you to double down on your position if you wish.

Stay Away From Overactivity

You won't need to check up on your stocks more than once every quarter, like when you receive quarterly reports. Still, it can be tempting to monitor your stocks continually and see how they are performing, but doing so can lead to overreacting to minor events in the short term. It can also make you feel as though you need to do something when really there's no need to act, and you end up focusing on the share price rather than the value of the company.

If and when one of your stocks goes through a sudden shift in price, try to figure out the cause. Has something changed business-wise for the company? Has your stock fallen victim to collateral damage caused by the market's response to an unrelated event? Or is it something that will influence your outlook on the long term in a meaningful way?

Short-term noise is very rarely relevant to how a well-chosen company will perform over the long term. Rather, it is how you, as an investor, reacts to the noise that truly matters. This is where your ability to think rationally and calmly comes into play, and when your investment plan will truly serve as a guide to holding out during the ebbs and flows of the stock market that are inevitable.

Evaluating a Stock

The reason that I consider stocks a long-term investment is because there is quite a lot of risk involved. You will need some time to weather any ebbs and flows and benefit from gains in the long term. Basically, stock investment is great for generating money that you won't be desperately needing in the next five years.

Collect research materials for your stock

Before you invest in a stock, you'll want to review the financials of the associated company. This is what is known as quantitative research, and begins with gathering a couple of documents that companies are required to file with the Securities and Exchange Commission in the US.

Form 10-K

This form is an annual report that includes all of the independently audited key financial statements. This form allows you to review the company's source of income, its balance sheet, the way that it manages its income, and its expenses and revenues.

Form 10-Q

This form is much more straightforward. It is merely a quarterly update on the company's financial results and its operations.

If you are short on time, you can always find highlights from the forms mentioned above and other essential financial ratios on the website of your brokerage firm, or on major financial news sites. This information is crucial, as it lets you compare the performance of one company against its competitors and other candidates for your investment.

Tighten Your Focus

The financial reports mentioned above contain dozens upon dozens of numbers and values, and it is very easy to become overwhelmed. That's why it is so important to focus on certain terms so that you can familiarize yourself with the inner workings of a company that is measurable.

Net Income

The net income of a company is called its *bottom-line* figure, since it is listed at the end of an income statement. Very creative. It is the total sum of money that a company is made after its operating expenses, depreciation and taxes have been deducted from the revenue. Revenue is the equivalent of your gross salary, while net income can be seen as what money you have left over after you have paid your taxes and rent.

Revenue

Revenue is the amount of cash that a company brings in during a specified period. It is the first thing you will see on an income statement and is thus referred to as the *top line* figure. Revenue can sometimes be categorized into *operating revenue* and *non-operating revenue.* Operating revenue is usually the most informative since it is generated from the core business of the company. Non-operating revenue usually comes from once-off business activities, like when an asset is sold.

Price-Earnings Ratio (P/E)

To determine the trailing P/E ratio of a company, you need to divide its current stock price by its earnings per share, generally over the last year. On the other hand, when you divide the stock price by the earnings predicted by Wall Street analysts, you're able to see the forward P/E of a company. This measure of the value of a stock can help you determine how much investors are willing to pay to receive $1 of a company's earnings.

Remember that the P/E ratio is divided from the earnings per share calculation that can potentially be flawed and estimates from analysts are usually focused on the short term. This means that it is not a very reliable metric on its own.

Earnings and Earnings Per Share (EPS)

Dividing a company's earnings by the number of available shares for trade, you receive the earnings per share. This value indicates how profitable a company is on the basis of per-share, making it far easier to compare with other competitor companies. When you notice that earnings per share value is followed by '(ttm)', it is referring to the 'trailing twelve months'.

This measurement is not even close to perfect since it does not provide an indication of how efficiently a company is making use of its capital. Some companies will take their earnings and pay them out to shareholders in dividends, while others might use them to reinvest in the business.

Return on Assets (ROA) and Return on Equity (ROE)

In terms of percentiles, the return on equity of a company reveals how much profit it is generating with each dollar that is invested by shareholders. The equity belongs to the shareholders. On the other hand, return on assets is an indication of the percentage of profits that a company makes with each dollar of its assets. Each of these values is determined by dividing the company's net annual income by one of the above measures.

These percentages will also inform you about how efficiently a company is making profits. You will need to be wary of the 'gotchas' here. A company has the ability to boost its return on equity artificially by buying shares back, thereby reducing the shareholder equity denominator. Likewise, taking on more debt, like taking more loans to finance property or increase inventory, will add to the amount in assets used to calculate return on assets.

This is plenty of information to absorb, and it's perfectly normal to feel slightly overwhelmed. Do your best to take in what we've stated above so that you'll be ready for the next chapter, in which we're going to discuss the process of making your first stock investment!

Chapter Four:

Making Your First Investment

Unfortunately, investing in the stock market is not as simple as going to a store to make a purchase. The process of buying stocks involves creating a brokerage account, adding funds, and doing your homework about which stocks you should buy before tapping the purchase button on your broker's app or website.

This chapter discusses all of the steps you need to take before buying your first stock, as well as how you should go about choosing stocks that are worth your time and money.

Find an Online Broker That Works for You

The method for choosing an online broker that suits you the best has changed slightly over the years. Most major brokers nowadays have eliminated commissions for trading, which results in cost being largely out of the question. This leaves you with two primary considerations when comparing brokers.

You need to think about if a broker is meeting your needs and requirements, and how easy it is for you to use their platform. The latter is sometimes more important, especially as a newer investor, as it makes entering the field more accessible.

Is your broker providing all you need?

An example of a good online broker would be one that offers some great learning resources for newer investors, stock research, and some other tools. Certain online brokers also offer face-to-face branches, for those who decide that they want some guidance in person.

Other notable features that could be beneficial include allowing investors to trade in foreign markets and allowing them to buy fractional stock shares. Not all brokers provide these features, so try to look out for the ones that do.

Is the platform easy to navigate and user-friendly?

Like I said earlier, this question is probably slightly more important for new investors, as jumping into a complex trading platform can be confusing and will often leave you feeling demotivated. If you decide that you are going to trade from your phone or tablet, you will want a mobile broker platform that is user-friendly enough for you.

Luckily, most of the popular brokers let you test their trading platforms out with virtual money before you actually sign up. This allows you to try a few out before deciding on one platform to trade with.

Open Your Brokerage Account, and Fund it

Once you have decided on a brokerage platform, you will need to complete a new account application. You will want to have your Social Security number and driver's license on hand, and your bank account details as well if you are going to fund your account from your personal savings account.

The sign-up process is generally quick and painless, and you'll have to make two decisions when completing an application.

Are you looking for options trading privileges?

As a new investor, it is better to stay away from options until you know what you are doing, and you are familiar with the stock market. There are generally a variety of options privileges that you can choose from, and you always have the option to apply for a change later on.

Are you looking for margin privileges?

Margin privileges essentially allow you to borrow money to use for buying more stocks. Even though investing on margin is not really ideal, having margin privileges can be beneficial sometimes. You usually are not able to use deposited funds until they are cleared, unless you have a margin account.

When it comes to actually funding your account, there are a few options available to you. Most people choose to use EFT, or electronic funds transfer, to deposit money into their account. Other common methods include wiring the money or mailing the brokerage a check.

Decide on Stocks to Buy

We've already talked about analyzing stocks and classifying them in the previous chapters, so, with that information in mind, it's time to determine which stock or stocks you want to buy into your new account. Remember to concentrate on the long term and acquire stock that you want to own for the next five or ten years. Do not only focus on stocks that you think will perform well in the next couple of months.

You also need to keep in mind how beneficial diversification is. You don't want to put all of your cash in only three or four stocks, even if you are starting your account with a small sum of money. Since trading has become mostly free of commissions, it is now more practical to purchase a couple of shares in several different stocks.

Choose an Order Type

You will have a few different types of orders to choose from, with 'market' orders being the best choice for investors looking at the long term. This lets you brokerage know that you wish to buy stocks right away, and at the best price possible.

Another pretty common type of order is called a 'limit' order. With this type of order, the broker knows the highest price that you are willing to pay. To give an example, you might want a stock that is currently trading for $22 per share, but you want to be able to buy it for less than $20. So, you're able to enter a limit order that tells your broker only to make the purchase if the price reaches a level that you desire.

After you have filled out your trade ticket and have pressed 'place order', it should take mere seconds for your broker to execute the order. Once that is done, the shares should show up on your account straight away.

Enter Your Orders

This is the final step in the process of buying your first stocks. You will need to place the order with your broker by entering the stock symbol of your choice, whether you are buying or selling shares, and the number of shares you want.

Then, all you need to do is observe as the long-term compounding ability of the market does all the work for you. You can usually enroll in the DRIP plan of your broker with the press of a button if you want your dividends to be reinvested into more shares automatically.

Like I said before, try not to check up on your stocks too often, as tempting as it may be. Of course, you should keep up to date with the latest news from your companies by subscribing to news and looking at the quarterly reports. Just don't panic and sell if your stocks go down slightly.

Likewise, if your stocks increase slightly, try not to cash out right away. The best way to accumulate wealth over a long period is to buy shares from good companies and keep them for as long as those companies are successful.

Now that we've gone over how to make your first investment, let's look at some of the stocks you can expect to find on the market:

Value Stocks

In the stock market, the idea of value investing is the belief that if you can analyze the finances of enough companies and fairly predict the prices of stocks, you will be able to find stocks that are undervalued and might make appealing investments. This approach was first developed by the famous British economist, Benjamin Graham.

Value investing is what made many successful investors wealthy, but it is not always easy to find undervalued stocks. An incredibly useful measurement is to look at a company's book value per share, which details the assets of a company in comparison to the current share price.

You will want to be extra careful when it comes to smaller businesses, since they are almost always riskier and more prone to volatility than other stocks with a more stable value. You should also be wary of any companies that have experienced a major shift in price recently, because such shifts and any news events associated with them may influence a number of valuation and ratio methods.

Blue-Chip Stocks

Blue-chip stocks refer to those that are part of companies that are not likely to be influenced by major negative news stories, and that are longtime market standbys. Even if they were to be faced with negative publicity, they are companies that are old enough and sturdy enough to bounce back without any hindrances.

Blue chips are excellent for new investors since they will usually shift predictably with the market, and are not at as much of a risk than most other stocks. Walmart is an excellent example of a blue-chip stock. They are a chain store with a history dating back to 1962, have a massive market cap of $339.72 billion, and are relatively stable in comparison to the market as a whole.

The company holds the number one spot on the Fortune 500 list as of 2019, with more than $500 billion in annual revenue. The Fortune 500, and other lists like it, are excellent places for new investors to track down blue-chip investments.

Below is a checklist for buying your first stock:

1. *Buy what you know*

2. *Understand how the company makes money*

3. *Understand how the company is measuring its growth*

4. *Recognize the risk factors and competition*

5. *Understand how the company is spending its free cash flow*

6. *See if the stock is cheap in relation to its peers and the market*

Chapter Five:

Profits, Profits, Profits!

You do not need to be hitting home runs to be successful in the stock market. Instead, you should focus on getting the base hits, and try to grow your portfolio by taking most gains in the range of 20%-25%. While it may sound counterintuitive, it is always best to sell stock when it's on the rise, consistently advancing and looking appealing to all other investors.

As you may have already figured out, trading on the stock market is a risky business, though the rewards that can come from these risks make it all worth it. Even though you will never be able to eliminate the risks completely, there are some things you can do to mitigate risks by actively managing your portfolio and making clever investments.

However, if you are not careful, or if you don't really know what you're doing, you could end up paying a pretty hefty price. The buy low and sell high strategy might have resulted in the success of many investors, but it is not how the real professionals become successful. Instead, smart investors deploy their money strategically in order to allow it to work in more ways than one. In layman's terms, they multitask their money.

In this chapter, we're going to look at some of the ways you can maximize your profits and get the most out of your investments.

Price Action Strategies

If you were to think of investing like a game, the way you would win would be to purchase a stock at a low price and then sell it later on at a higher price. If you are a homeowner, then you likely understand this concept quite practically. It's best to use one of two strategies to make a profit on your investment.

The first is known as **value investing**, which relates to the **value stocks** mentioned in the previous chapter. Like the products you buy from stores each and every day, stocks go on sale every now and then, and value investors wait for this sale to happen. This makes it easier for them to make a profit, since stocks that are undervalued, or *on sale,* have more room for growth.

Unfortunately, your favorite stock might not be suited to this strategy since it has to pay a dividend. It would need to have a price low enough for you to be able to buy 100 shares, and it needs to trade many shares every day - at least 1 million shares of daily volume is preferable. Keep in mind that the value of a company is not based on its price.

There are many high-quality stocks that trade for $100 or more, and stocks that cost between $15 and $30, with a dividend yield of at least 2%, are the most favorable. You also want to avoid stocks that are highly volatile, as their more unpredictable shifts in price are more difficult to manage. This is where your stock evaluation skills and research will be put to the test.

Once you have found your stock, and you have decided that you want to value invest, you want this name to be in the middle or near the bottom of the trading range for the last 52 weeks. If it is not currently there, then you should either find another company or just wait for the stock to be at a price you are willing to pay for.

The second strategy is known as **momentum trading.** Some investors believe that the best time for a stock to be bought is when it's price continues to rise, since, as we learned in school, objects in motion tend to remain in motion. The only problem with this strategy is that it is usually only beneficial to short-term investors. Most people want to think of the long term, as the longer you are in possession of stock, the better its potential returns can be.

Invest for Dividends

In the world of high-tech stock trading, it is often considered boring to invest for dividends, but they can truly be a major source of income for long-term investors. Dividends provide us with two distinct advantages that help us get our money working in more ways than one. First, they provide a stable income. Even though companies may choose to pay or not to pay dividends, companies of higher qualities and with lower payout ratios have a lower chance of cutting your quarterly dividend payment.

Let's use an example to put things into perspective. You've done your research and have decided to buy shares in stock *XYZ*. You purchased 100 shares at $30 each, which had a 3% dividend yield at the time.

$$\$3\,000 \text{ x } 3\% = \$90 \quad \text{annually}$$

You are not only making $90 every year, but because a dividend is paid to your account as cash, you can apply that payment of dividends to what you paid for the stock for each year you own the 100 shares. In this case, you can also subtract 90 cents per share. After only five years, the stock that once cost you $30 per share will go down to $25.50 per share. Many long-term investors are able to reduce the price that they paid for stock to $0 from the dividend alone.

Make Use of Covered Calls

Covered calls are slightly more complex. If you are not confident with this kind of strategy, using the method of purchasing a stock and collecting its dividend as it increases will still provide you with some significant gains. You need to ask yourself two important questions before you sell a covered call:

What is the strike price?

How many months do you want your contract to last for?

Strike price

Covered calls are a kind of options contract strategy that allows the contract holder to purchase your 100 shares, if it is at the strike price or above it. You probably do not want someone to take your shares from you, though you might have a change of heart later in your career, so the strike price will need to be steep enough that the stock does not rise above it, but low enough that you will still be able to collect a decent premium for taking a risk.

This is a pretty tough decision to make, especially for new investors such as yourself. If your stock is currently experiencing a downtrend, you will likely be able to sell an option with a strike price not much higher than the current actual price of the stock. If the stock is experiencing an uptrend, however, you may want to wait until you are happy that the move up has run its course, and that the stock will soon shift in the opposite direction. Remember that whenever a stock appreciates in value, your option value depreciates.

Expiration date

The further you take your option into the future, the bigger your premium payout will be upfront, to sell the call, but that also means more time that your stock needs to be below the strike price, to avoid it being 'called away' from you. Consider going three or four months ahead for your first contract.

As soon as you sell it, your covered call will make money for you, since the premium that is paid by the buyer will be deposited into your account directly. It will keep making money for you even if your stock's price drops. The premium falls with the price. You are able to buy back the contract from the buyer at any time, so, if the premium does fall, you can buy it for less than what you sold it for.

That means you're making a profit. At the same time, if your stock were to rise above the strike price, you would be able to buy the contract for more than you sold it, causing a loss, but also saving you needing to hand over 100 of your shares. One of the most effective ways to use the covered call is to collect the premium right at the beginning.

Even though you can buy the option back if its price shifts, you will want to only do so under dire circumstances. You should also keep in mind that the money you collect from selling your covered call can also be deducted from the price you paid for the stock.

The easiest way to get the hang of a new investment strategy is to make use of a virtual platform, like the ones many brokerage firms offer in their apps or websites. You are still able to buy the stock and collect dividends but wait to sell the covered call until you feel that you are comfortable with the way it works.

Chapter Six:

Knowing When to Sell

The money-making process with stocks involves two crucial decisions - knowing when it's the right time to buy, and when it's the right time to sell. You have to have both of them right to be able to make profits. Generally, there are three good reasons as to why you should sell a stock:

1. The price of the stock has increased drastically

2. The stock has reached a price that is no longer sustainable

3. Buying the stock in the first place was a mistake

In this chapter, we are going to look at these reasons in more detail and discuss their implications.

Buying Right

The first thing used to determine the return on any investment is its purchase price. You could argue that a loss or profit is made the second that it is purchased - the buyer just won't know until it has been sold. Even though buying at the correct price might determine the profit made in the end, selling at the right price will *guarantee* that a profit is made. If you do not sell at the correct time, the benefits you had from buying at the right time could fall away.

Selling Stock is Difficult

Many investors have a hard time selling stocks, and it has a lot to do with our greedy nature as humans. Let's give a common scenario:

You purchase a share of stocks for $25, and intend to sell it, if and when it reaches $30. It hits $30, so you then decide to wait a bit longer for a few more points. The stock then reaches $33, and soon your greed overpowers your ability to think rationally. Suddenly, the price of the stock drops down to $28, and you tell yourself to wait again until it's back at $30. This will never happen, and you will finally give in to your frustrations and sell it when it drops to $24.

Greed and emotion can very easily overcome your rational thinking, as you can see. You will have treated the stock market the same way you would a slot machine and lost. To remove human error from the equation for future decisions, try using a limit order, which will sell the stock automatically once it has reached your target price. You won't even need to monitor the performance of that stock - you'll just receive a notification when the sell order is placed.

When the Purchase Was a Mistake

If you are a diligent investor, you probably did some research into a stock before you bought it. At a later stage, you might realize that you had made an analytical error that affects the suitability for a business as an investment in a fundamental way. You should then sell the stock, even if it has to be at a loss.

The key to being a successful investor is to rely on your analysis and data rather than the emotional mood swings of the stock market. If your analysis, for any reason, turns out to be flawed, sell the stock and move forward. The price of the stock could increase after you've sold it, which can make you second guess yourself. Or a 10% loss on that particular investment might be the smartest decision you have ever made.

Obviously, not all analytical errors are the same. If a business does not meet your predictions for the short term, and the price of the stock decreases, do not overreact and sell if the integrity of the business remains the same. However, if you do notice that the company is losing market share to its competitors, it could be a sign of weakness in the long term and would constitute a good reason to sell.

When the Stock Experiences a Drastic Rise

It is not impossible for your stock to rise significantly in a short period for any number of reasons. The best investors are those that are the most humble. Do not assume that a rise is an affirmation that you are smarter than the market itself. Instead, sell.

Cheap stocks can become expensive stocks very quickly for a wide variety of reasons, including the speculation of others. Rather take your gains and move on. Even better, if a stock suddenly drops, consider buying it again.

Sell for Valuation

This decision for selling is part scientific, part artistic. Ultimately, the value of a stock rests on the current value of the future cash flows of a company. Since the future is uncertain, the valuation will always be, to some extent, imprecise. This is why the majority of value investors very heavily rely on the margin of safety concepts when investing.

It is generally always a good idea to consider selling if the valuation of a company reaches a significantly higher level than that of its peers. This rule does have many exceptions, though, which is what makes it so complex. For example, if *Company A* is trading for 15 times earnings, and *Company B* is trading for 13 times earnings, then there is no reason that you should not sell *Company A* when considering the sizable market share of their products.

Another selling tool that is slightly more reasonable is to sell when the P/E ratio of a company exceeds its own average P/E ratio for the last 7-10 years significantly. To give another example, Walmart shares had a 60 times earnings P/E at the height of the internet boom. Despite the quality of the company, any investors who owned shares in Walmart should have and could have considered selling, and prospective buyers should have thought of looking elsewhere.

When the revenue of a company drops, it is usually an indication that the demand has decreased. You should first look at the annual revenue figure in order to get a look at the bigger picture, but you should not rely on these numbers alone. Take a look at the quarterly figures too. The numbers of annual revenue for a major gas and oil company could be impressive on an annual basis, but what if energy prices have dropped in the last few months?

When you notice that a company is cutting costs, it usually means that said company is not thriving. The most telling indicator for this is a reduced headcount. The good news, for you at least, is that initially, cutting costs will be seen as a positive, which tends to lead to stock gains. Though you should not view this as an opportunity to acquire more shares, but instead as a way to leave the position before the inevitable plummet in value.

Selling Because of Financial Requirements

This reason may not be 'valid' from an analytical point of view, but it is still a reason. Stocks are, at the end of the day, assets, and there are sometimes where people will have to cash in on their assets. Whether the money will be used as capital for a new business, purchasing a new home, or paying for college tuition, the decision is entirely dependent on your financial situation, rather than the fundamentals of the stock market.

Rebalancing Your Portfolio

Sometimes, you may decide that your portfolio is not diverse in the way that you wish it was. This is a perfectly valid reason to sell a stock or several stocks, and there are two situations where this could be a necessity.

Reducing stock exposure

As you grow older and draw closer to your retirement, it is a good idea to reduce your stock exposure gradually. Even though stocks do have great potential for returns in the long term, they are, as you know, quite volatile, and preservation of capital becomes more and more important as you get closer to retiring. One good rule is to subtract your current age from 110 to get the percentage of your current portfolio that you should invest in the stock market. If it's been a couple of years since the last time you adjusted your allocation of assets, it may be a good thought to sell some of your holdings in stocks and put the money into bonds.

High-performance stocks

Sometimes, your stocks perform well. Very well. So well, in fact, that it seems unreasonable to have so much money invested in a single company. In this case, it is a good idea to sell, so that the wealth of your portfolio can be distributed more evenly across more companies.

The Company Has Been Acquired

When the acquisition of a company is announced, the price for the stocks of the company being acquired will usually rise to a level that is similar to the agreed-upon price. Nine times out of ten, it is a wise idea to lock in your gains, as the upside potential is usually pretty limited. There are three ways that a company can be potentially acquired -stock, cash, or both.

In a cash-only acquisition, the stock will usually move toward the price of acquisition. It is rarely worth holding onto your shares in this type of acquisition, as there is no real upside for having your money tied up for months, and if the deal were to collapse, your shares could plummet.

With stock or cash-and-stock acquisition, it can be slightly more complex, and your decision will have to come down to whether or not you want to be a shareholder in the company that is making the acquisition. If not, it is perfectly reasonable to cash out.

In the next chapter, we're going to look at how you should be managing your stock portfolio as a new investor and some of the things you can do to make managing your investment portfolio easier and more efficient.

Chapter Seven:

Managing Your Stock Portfolio

Too many young people very rarely invest for retirement, if ever. Some far away date, like 40 or 50 years into the future, is difficult for many new, young investors to comprehend. But, without investments to supplement income during retirement, if you have any at all, prospective investors will likely find it difficult to make it pay for the necessities.

Investments that are disciplined, smart, and made on a regular basis in a portfolio with holdings that are diverse can yield some great returns in the long term. One of the primary reasons that young people do not invest is that they do not understand stocks fully or fail to wrap their heads around basic concepts like the power of compounding and the time value of money. Luckily, these things are not difficult to learn, and you're holding in your hands the best resource out there to learn them.

You need to start investing early. The sooner you start, the more time that your investments will have to grow and compound. Most of the investment industry involves making things sound more complicated than they are so that you feel inadequate enough to let an 'expert' control your money.

Of course, trustworthy advice from an advisor with a good reputation will always be useful, the simple truth is that paying exorbitant prices for professional investment management will not automatically guarantee superior investment return, especially once you have your fees accounted for. Proactive investors who want to take their destiny into their own hands will be glad to hear that it is not very difficult at all to build a portfolio and manage it using the same techniques that the pros do.

Let's look at how you should manage your investment portfolio.

Learn Some Simple Principles of Investing

As you may have learned from *Chapter Two,* there are a wide variety of investment strategies out there, and some of them can be quite daunting and intimidating. Even though using a complication system that requires plenty of attention, information, and time might work perfectly well for some folks, they are not needed to be a successful investor. Using one of the strategies that was mentioned in *Chapter Two* will be more than adequate, since they are not very complicated, but are still super effective.

Start Early

As soon as you start working and earning money, you should begin saving by participating in a 401(k) retirement plan, if your employer offers it. If there is no 401(k) available, establish an IRA, or Individual Retirement Account and earmark a percentage of your compensation for a contribution to your account each month. Creating an automatic cash contribution that goes off each month is a very convenient and efficient way to save a 401(k) or IRA.

Try to remember that savings accumulate, and your interest will compound without taxes only for so long as you do not withdraw the money. This means that it would be wise to establish one of these investment vehicles early in your working career.

Early Higher Risk Allocation

Another good reason to start saving your money early is that the younger you are, the less likely it is for you to become burdened with financial obligations, like children, a spouse, or a mortgage, to name but a few. Without these burdens in your life, you are able to allocate some of your investment portfolio to investments that have a higher risk, which will often return greater yields.

Also, when you begin investing as a young person, before you start accumulating financial commitments, you will likely have more cash available to invest, and a much greater period of time before your retirement.

You will have a greater retirement *nest egg* with more money to invest, for years and years to come.

Exemplary Eggs

Let's illustrate the advantage of investing as soon as you are able. Assume that, every month, you invest $200 from the age of 25. If you are earning an annual return on that money of 7%, when you reach the age of 65, your retirement nest egg is going to be somewhere around $525,000.

However, if you only start saving that $200 each month when you are 35 years old, and still receive the same return of 7%, then you will only have about $244,000 when you are 65 years old. For those who start investing only later in their lives, there are some tax advantages available. Notably, 401(k) plans allow for *catch-up contributions* for folks that are 50 years and older. IRAs do this as well.

Diversify

You've read it time and time again throughout this guide, but you should always select stocks across a wide range of market categories. The most effective way to do this is via an index fund. You should try to invest in stocks that are conservative, and have regular dividends, as well as stocks that have a potential to grow in the long term, and a small number of stocks that have a better risk potential or can provide better returns.

If you are investing in stocks individually, avoid putting more than 4% of your total portfolio into one stock. This will prevent your portfolio from being affected adversely if one or two stocks suffer a drastic downturn. Some AAA-rated bonds can also be excellent investments for the long term, either government or corporate.

Keep Your Costs as Low as Possible

It is always a good idea to invest with a discount brokerage firm. Another reason for you to consider index funds as a new investor is that their fees are usually quite low. Since you are (probably) going to be investing for the long term, you should do your best to avoid buying and selling regularly in response to short term market ups and downs. This will save you some expenses for commission and management fees, which might prevent losses in cash when your stock price declines.

Investing Regularly and Being Discipline

Ensure that you are putting your money into your investments regularly and in a disciplined manner. This might not be possible if you were to become unemployed, but once you have secured another job, you will be able to continue to fund your portfolio.

Take Your Time

You do not need to rush when selecting a portfolio or implementing one. When you have settled on a portfolio that you are happy with, sleep on it before making any other decisions. In fact, you should wait at least a few months before making another move. Buyer's remorse is totally normal when you are returning an item to a store, but exchanging a portfolio has some major implications when it comes to tax. You will need to be clever about your decisions and to act with as little emotion as possible.

When you are just entering the stock market industry, you should try not to stress about having your portfolio implemented perfectly right away. A good way to start any portfolio would be to buy a large cap index fund or a total stock market, since it will act as a main component for pretty much all other asset allocations that you grow into.

As you accumulate more money and become more educated as to the inner workings of the stock market, you will be able to look at newer, more exciting assets and diversify your holdings and move towards an asset allocation goal set in the long term.

Rebalance Every Year

The best way you could manage your portfolio is to ignore it, despite the impression that you might be getting from financial news outlets. Keep in mind that you are already much better off than many other investors, since you have already decided on an asset allocation, and are paying close attention to its volatility and returns historically. You can rest easy knowing that you have made a well-educated decision.

Markets fluctuate constantly, and your allocation of assets will do its job passively, while also growing and protecting your money without you needing to monitor it constantly. However, you will need to check up on your money once a year to see if any of your assets have shifted from your target percentages.

If they have, then you are going to need to rebalance. There are two ways in which you can do this. The first is to use new money that you have accumulated and saved over the year and purchase shares of the funds that have dipped below the price you were aiming for. Alternatively, you could sell the shares of the funds that performed the best and use the money to acquire more shares of those that did not.

About Taxes

You should always remember that if you are investing in an account that can be taxed, so one that is not a 401(k) or an IRA, then selling funds is going to impact your taxes. I recommend buying shares with new money first before you sell anything. When you do have to sell, make sure that you understand the tax implications of any change before it is made.

This may sound quite daunting, but think of it positively. There are many ways that you can reduce tax by managing your own portfolio smartly, in ways that other investors who are giving their portfolio choices to others are not able to. If you are still confused, it may be beneficial to see a tax advisor. However, once you have gone through the process once or twice, you will get the hang of it in no time.

Life Goes On

It's really as simple as finding an appropriate portfolio that suits you, purchasing the index funds that you need from a brokerage account, and rebalancing once every year. You have complete control over your portfolio, and you certainly have the ability to manage it using the methods for asset allocation from respected experts. It's much easier than it sounds.

Chapter Eight:
Analyzing the Market

You're never asked to be your own lawyer or doctor, so why should you be obligated to be your own stock market analyst? Some people take up cooking merely because it is something that they enjoy. Likewise, there are folks who enjoy the process of making investments. Therefore, if you are the type of investor that enjoys being independent and self-reliant, then you should certainly consider becoming your own stock analyst.

Some analysts have a question mark hovering over their credibility rating, so it is always better to get the hang of analysis on your own. That's what we'll be discussing in this chapter.

Trust the Stock Analysis Process

Regardless of whether you are an investor looking for value or growth, developing your mind is the first step you need to take toward thinking like an analyst. You need to figure out what to sell and what to buy, and at what price. Analysts will generally focus on a certain sector or industry. Within that industry, they'll focus on a certain few companies.

The goal of an analyst is to deeply inspect the affairs of each of the companies on their list. This is done by analyzing their financial statements and all other information from the company that they can get their hands on. In order to cross-examine the facts, analysts will also inspect the companies' suppliers, competitors, and customers, and their affairs.

Some analysts will also visit a company and interact with its management so that they can understand first-hand of the company. Over time, professional analysts will connect all the dots to get a good view of the bigger picture. Before you make any sort of investment, you need to do your own research. It's always more beneficial to research into several stocks of the same industry so that your analysis can be comparative.

Accessing this information generally is not a problem. The biggest issue that you might face when trying to become your own stock market analyst is time. Retail investors who are busy with a number of other projects at once might not be able to allocate as much time as a professional security analyst might.

But, you are definitely able to take just a couple of firms from the start, to test how well you are able to analyze them. Doing so will help you understand the process, and, with more time and experience, you can think about inspecting and analyzing more and more stocks.

Start Where You Are

The best way to start your own analysis is to look over other analyst reports. That way, you can save much more time by cutting down the amount of preliminary work you need to do. You do not need to blindly buy or follow the recommendations that other analysts make.

Instead, you should read their research reports so that you can have a quick overview of the company, including its main competitors, strengths, weaknesses, future prospects, and industry outlook.

Analyst reports are packed full of useful information, and reading these reports made by various analysts at the same time will help you identify any similarities. Opinions might vary, but the basic facts in all of the reports should be common. Additionally, you can also look more closely at the earnings forecasts that different analysts create, which ultimately determine their buy and sell recommendations.

Different analysts might set different target prices for the same stock. You should always look for the reasons while you are studying the analyst reports. What would have *your* opinion been regarding the present stock given the same information? No idea? Look at the next heading.

What Should You Analyze?

You are going to have to understand the various steps involved in the process of stock analysis if you want to arrive at your own reliable conclusion about a stock. Some analysts will use the *top-down* strategy, starting with a certain industry, then locating a winning company. Others will follow a *bottom-up* approach, in which they start with a particular company and then inspect the outlook of the industry. You do not need to use any of these strategies, and you are at liberty to create your own order, so long as the entire process flows smoothly.

Analyzing an Industry

There are sources available to the public for almost any industry. The annual report of a company itself often provides a good enough overview of the industry that it belongs to, along with its predictions for growth in the future. Annual reports can also provide some information about the minor and major competitors in any particular industry.

Reading the reports from two or three companies at the same time will usually give you a clear picture. You could also subscribe to websites and trade magazines that cater to a certain industry for monitoring the latest events in that industry.

Analyzing Business Models

You need to be able to determine the strengths and weaknesses of a company and be able to focus on them. There can be a weak company in a strong industry, and a strong company in a weak industry. A company's strengths are usually reflected in things like its products, suppliers, customers, and unique brand identity. You can learn about the business model of a company from its annual report, websites, and trade magazines.

Financial Strength

Understanding a company's financial strength is the most crucial step to analyzing a stock, whether you like it or not. Without being able to understand the financials, you are not going to be able to think like an analyst. You should be able to understand a company's income statement, balance sheet, and cash flow statements.

Usually, the figures lying in the financial statements are more meaningful than the glossy words written in an annual report. If you are not comfortable with numbers, but you want to be able to analyze stocks, then there is no time like right now to start familiarizing yourself with them.

Quality of Management

This is another crucial factor for any stock analyst. You may have heard that there are no good or bad companies, but only good or bad managers - the key executives that are responsible for the future of the company. You can assess the management of a company and the quality of its board by doing a bit of research on the internet. There is a multitude of information out there about every public company.

Analysis of Growth

Stock prices follow earnings, so if you want to know whether the price of a stock is going to move upward or downward in the future, then you will need to know where the future earnings are going. Unfortunately, there is no simple formula that you will be able to use to know what to expect for future earnings. Analysts generally make their own estimates by looking at the past figures for growth of sales and profit margins, as well as a particular industry's profitability trends.

Essentially, it connects what has occurred in the past to what is predicted to happen in the future. If you are able to make earnings forecasts that are accurate enough, you will be able to assess your abilities as a stock analyst, since it is a clear indication of your understanding of those companies and industries.

Chapter Nine:
Mistakes to Avoid

Failure is a part of the learning process of investing and trading. As an investor, you will usually be involved in holdings in the long term and will trade in stocks, other securities, and exchange-traded funds. Traders usually sell and buy future options, are involved in a higher number of transactions, and hold their positions for shorter periods.

Even though investors and traders make use of two different kinds of trading transactions, they are often responsible for making nearly identical mistakes. Some of these mistakes can be more detrimental to investors, while others can be more detrimental to traders. Both traders and investors will be better off to remember these common mistakes and how they can be avoided.

Failing to Plan

Every experienced trader enters the industry with a plan that has been carefully thought out. They know their exact points of exit and entry, the maximum loss that they are willing to take, and the amount of capital that they need to invest in the trade. Beginner traders might not have a plan to follow before they begin trading.

Even if they do have a plan, they might still be more likely to shift away from their established plan than more experienced traders would. Novice traders might even change their course completely. For example, you might go short after you had initially bought securities since the share price is dropping, and only end up being whipsawed.

Clutching Performance

Numerous traders and investors will choose strategies, classes, funds, and managers based on a relevant strong performance. The feeling of missing out on returns has likely led to more bad investment decisions than most other investment factors. If a certain strategy, asset class, or fund has performed very well for four or five years, you can know one thing for sure: you should have invested four or five years ago. Now, the specific cycle that caused that good performance is probably drawing to a close. The smart money is heading out.

Not Regaining Balance

As we discussed in a previous chapter, the process of getting your portfolio back to its desired allocation of assets, as outlined in your investment plan, is known as rebalancing. Rebalancing can be difficult since it might force you to sell the asset class that is doing the best and buy more assets from a class that is not performing well.

This contrarian action is quite challenging for many new investors. However, portfolios that are left to drift with the market return will guarantee that asset classes will be overweight at market peaks and underweight at the lows of the market - a recipe for bad performance. Rebalance religiously and receive the rewards in the long term.

Ignoring Aversions to Risk

You have to continually keep track of your risk tolerance, or the capacity you have to take risks. Many investors can't handle the ups and downs and volatility that is linked to the stock market or other trades that are more speculative. Other investors might need a secure source of regular interest income. These investors with a low tolerance for risk will be well off investing in the blue-chip stocks from established businesses rather than the more volatile startup and growth company shares.

Always keep in mind that any investment return has a risk attached to it. The investments with the lowest risk are those in US treasury bills, bonds, and notes. There are many types of investments from there that move up the ladder of risk and can also offer greater returns as compensation for the higher risk that they make you take on.

If an investment offers a very appealing return, you should also inspect the risk profile that is attached to it and how much money you might lose if things were to go south. Never invest more than you can afford to lose.

Neglecting Your Time Frame

You should never invest without having a time frame in mind. Think about whether or not you are going to need the money that you are pouring into an investment before you enter the trade. You should also decide how long - called the *time horizon* - you will need to save for your retirement, college education, a down payment for your home, or your children.

If you plan to accumulate wealth to purchase a house, it can be thought of as more of a medium-term time frame. But, if you invest with the plan of financing a college tuition, then you could view it as more of a long-term investment. If you are saving for your retirement, which is thirty years from now, then what happens in the market this year or the next should not be one of your major concerns. Once you have a grasp of your horizon, you will be able to track down investments that fit its profile and frame.

Not Making Use of Stop-Loss Orders

This is one of the biggest signs that you do not have a plan. There are a wide variety of stop orders available, and they are all able to limit losses that are caused by adverse movements in stock, or by the stock market as wholly. These orders are automatically executed once the parameters that you have set have been met.

Tight stops usually entail that your losses will be capped before that can become extreme. But, there is the risk that stop orders on long positions might be carried out at levels below what you have specified, should there be a sudden lowering of the security gap, which happened to several inventors during the Flash Crash.

Even with this thought in mind, the risks of stopping out at a price that was not planned is far outweighed by the benefits that stop orders provide. A corollary to this mistake that traders make is when a trader cancels a stop order on losing a trade right before it can be caused because they think that the trend in price could reverse.

Allowing Your Losses to Accumulate

One of the greatest aspects of successful traders and investors is how they are able to speedily take a small loss if a trade does not go according to plan, and progress to their next trading idea. On the other hand, less successful traders can become immobilized with fear if a trade counters their plans.

They might hold on to a losing position instead of raking fast action to cap the loss, in the hopes that the trade may eventually work out. A losing trade can end up having your trade capital tied up for a long time, and could result in severe depletion of capital and mounting losses.

Averaging Up or Down

Averaging down in a blue-chip stock on a long position might work out for investors with a long-term investment horizon, but it might lead to something rather unfortunate for traders who are trading securities that are more volatile and come with greater risks. Some of the greatest trading failures in the history of the market have taken place because a trader kept adding to a position that was losing, and eventually had to cut the position entirely when the extent of the loss became unreasonable.

Traders also go short frequently, more so than investors who are more conservative, and will usually average up, since the security is advancing instead of retreating. This is just as risky and is another regular mistake that many new investors make.

Not Knowing When to Accept Your Losses

Investors all too often fail to accept the plain fact that they are only human and that they are going to make mistakes - just like the great investors. Whether one of your longtime big earners has suddenly taken a bad turn, or you hastily made a stock purchase, the best thing you should do is accept your losses.

The worst thing to do would be to let your pride cloud your thinking and maintain an investment that is clearly losing. Or, even worse, purchase more of the stock since it is now cheaper. You would be surprised as to how often this mistake is made, and those who do make it do it by comparing the 52-week high of the stock with the current share price. Many folks that use this gauge assume that share prices that share prices that have fallen represent good purchases. But, there was a reason that the drop happened in the first place, and it is up to you to analyze why it happened.

Falling for False Buy Signals

The resignation of a CEO, deteriorating fundamentals, or heightened competition are all plausible causes for stock to lower in price. These very same conditions also provide some great clues to indicate that the stock may not increase soon. A company could be worthless at the moment for fundamental reasons, and it is essential that you always maintain a keen eye, as a low price for shares could also be a false buy signal.

You should never buy stocks in the bargain basement. There is a compelling fundamental reason for a decline in price in most cases. Instead, do your research and analyze the outlook of a stock before you decide to invest. You will want to invest in companies that are going to experience sustained growth in the years to come. The future operating performance of a company has very little to do with the price that you bought its shares.

Making a Purchase With Too Much Margin

Margin is using money that you have borrowed from your broker to acquire securities, often options and futures. Even though margins can aid you in more money, they can also increase your losses by just as much, if not more. You should ensure that you have a good understanding of how margin works, and how your broker might require you to sell any positions that you already have.

The worst thing a new investor or trader could do is get carried away with what feels like free money. If you are using margin and your investment does not go as planned, you could have a hefty debt obligation for nothing. Ask yourself if you would buy stocks using your credit card. You wouldn't. Excessively using margin is basically the same thing, usually just at a lower rate of interest.

Additionally, when you use margin, you will have to keep a much keener eye on your positions. Exaggerated losses and gains that come with the small movements in price can cause disaster. If you do not have the knowledge or time to constantly monitor your positions and make decisions about them, and their values drop, your broker will sell your stock to cover any of your losses.

Use margin sparingly as a new trader, if you use it at all, and only use it once you understand the risks that are associated. It can force you to sell all of your positions at the bottom, which is the point that you should be in the market for a big turnaround.

Herd Mentality

This is also another very commonly made mistake by new investors. They blindly obey the herd and might end up paying too much for popular stocks or might initiate short positions in securities that have already plummeted and could be on the verge of turning around. Even though more experienced traders follow the mantra that the trend is your friend, it is because they are used to leaving trades when they become overcrowded.

However, new traders might stay in a trade after the smart money has left it. They could also lack the confidence needed to take an approach that is contrary to the trend when it is required of them.

Too Much Financial Television

This last one might seem quite silly, but there is pretty much nothing that financial news can offer you that will help you reach your goals. There are hardly any newsletters that could give you anything valuable, and even if there were, how would you be able to identify them in advance?

If someone truly did have trading advice, profitable stock tips, or the secret formula to making it big, would they talk about it on TV or sell it to you for $50 a month? Nope. They would keep it to themselves, make their millions, and then have absolutely no need to sell a newsletter to make their living.

So what's the solution? Stop watching so much financial television and reading newsletters. Spend more time curating your investment plan and sticking to it.

Wrapping Up

You've made it to the end! Congrats! You have just taken your first step towards becoming a successful investor in the stock market. Hopefully, you were able to learn a couple of things from this guide that will help you achieve your financial success in the future. Be sure to refer back to the chapters in this guide if you need any advice during your career.

Happy trading!

The Day Trading

Day Trading

Nowadays, the trading topic is taking the world by storm and more and more people are willing to try out themselves in the role of a trader. There exist plenty of myths around this profession and the major part of people believe that in order to master this profession you need to have higher economic education or possess an over-developed intuition. Yes, there are such statements. A lot of people consider trading to be a game. In general, we are going to dispel the most common myths and provide answers to the following questions:

"How to become a trader from scratch?" and "who can become a trader?".

If you have a strong willing to become a trader, you don't need to have a higher education. No supplementary knowledge of mathematics or any other science is needed. Though, the ability to calculate quickly will come in handy. A trader has to know at what price to enter, where to put a stop, how to calculate the arithmetic average or percentage of perceived risk, etc. A future trader has to learn how to do it rapidly as there is a risk of entering at not the best price. Particularly, it is topical for scalping and intraday trading.

If you plan to be involved in long-term investing wherein fundamental analysis is more significant than a technical one, higher education won't be superfluous but it also will not give you any significant advantage. Traders are not taught at universities or institutes. You can master this craft by yourself or under the guidance of more seasoned and successful trader.

If you are a trader to be you should take into account, the following tips:

The primary quality of a trader is a stable psyche. This is the field where discipline and psychology take precedence. You must learn to keep your emotions under control, abide the trading system rules, and money management. It appears to be not so simple as at first sight. There is nothing for you to do in trading if you are a gambler. Most of the people do not understand the whole importance of controlling their emotions until they are engaged in the trading process. Therefore, it is worth trying. After giving it try, make a measured conclusion whether this profession is your thing or not. Another myth to be dispelled is that the developed intuition is a must for trading. Intuition doesn't belong to trading.

Trading is not a game, but a serious business where you need to stick to a distinct plan and algorithm, soberly assess the current situation on the market. If you trade relying only on your intuition and carry out non-systematic transactions, you will definitively suffer setback.

In addition, such personal qualities as industriousness, perseverance, patience, spirit, and flexibility of thinking, that is, the ability to think outside the box, are also of great importance for the trader who only starts his way.

The second prerequisite is the presence of some capital. You need to have some funds to open the account. Trading is one of those types of businesses where huge start-up capital is not necessary. Most people start trading by investing 100-200 dollars and try to disperse the deposit while increasing risks. This is the way to failure.

It must be taken into account that a very good income is 5-7% per month, considering this, calculate the sum of money on the account to make profit adequately without violating the money management.

The next point is the presence of free time. The more time you make for trading the faster you will show results.

Usually, trading does not take a lot of time, it is more significant to track the very entry point, and for the sake of this, you will have to carry out market analysis, select tools, and expect for the signal. If you don't have a lot of free time, then many entry points will be missed. However, this does not mean that you won't make the grades, the most important thing here is the transactions quality and compliance with the system. May there will be very few deals, but they will be of high quality and in accordance with the system. At this point, it is quite real to gain some profitability.

Some people find it difficult to expect. Even if you have found spare time and you started dealing with charts hoping to carry out some deals but it doesn't mean that the entry point will be formed on the spot. It seems to many people that they are frittering their time away, this leads to unsystematic transactions, which gives a deplorable result. A trader can spend several days not making a deal, if there is no appropriate entry signal.

Alternatively, you can conduct analysis on your laptop at home and then monitor these tools on your phone. In some cases, it will already allow to trade outside the home. There are some mobile applications with a terminal for smartphones. It is impossible to carry analysis of something on the phone in a meaningful way, the application only suits for tracking open positions. It also helps not to miss a specific tool signal that you have selected earlier.

Conclusion

Every person can become a trader or at least give it a shot. So, if you have taken fancy in this profession, you are willing to learn something new, give it a try for sure, maybe just you will become successful in this area and make a living for yourself. Keep in mind no pain no gain! If you approach the matter initially wisely, study this area properly, comprehend what money management is, then the risks are minimal.

Get ready for a time-consuming and difficult journey, as making money is not a simple way. However, if you really strive for this, have the necessary features and are ready to achieve your goal, then keep your eyes on the prize and everything will definitely work out.

Good luck!

Day Trading Basics

Day trading is the purchase and sale of financial instruments during one trading day. It can take place in any marketplace but the most popular are forex – foreign exchange and stock markets. Day traders are well-educated and well-funded. High amounts of leverage and short-term trading techniques are used to capitalize on minor market fluctuations in highly liquid commodities or currencies.

Day traders are set on events causing short-term market moves. Currently, news trading is in demand. Scheduled reports such as economic figures, corporate income, or interest rates are subject to consumer preferences and financial psychology. When those expectations are not lived up or are exceeded then market reacts, usually with abrupt, considerable moves, which can be the benefit for day traders.

Day traders apply several intraday strategies. These strategies include:

- Range trading primarily provides the support and resistance levels to define buy and sell decisions

- High-frequency trading (HFT) strategies use advanced algorithms to seize small or short-term market failures.

- Scalping (aimed at making numerous slight profits on small prices moves within the day)

- News-based trading, (typically uses trading opportunities from the increased volatility around news events)

Working with day trading strategies allows you to learn how to analyze the state of the market quickly, helps understand all the features of trading and to master all types of Forex analysis in a short time. This is partly why day trading is so popular among beginners. However, the shortest transactions of this type also require some practical knowledge and their own experience from a novice speculator.

When trading on short trades, the day trader can use any trading tools that he will like:

- Currency

- Liquid shares of companies

- Indices

- Precious metals

- Oil

- Futures

- Options

- Bonds

Thus, making small, but quite frequent transactions, the trader has the opportunity to better understand the process of trading, at the same time without losing a lot. In this case, the profit will be, although small (within the framework of one transaction), but regular.

Day trading advantages

- The day trader is able to control all of his risks easily

- There are no gaps in the work

- Such a speculator will always find what it is profitable for him to trade at the moment.

- Always convenient leverage available

- There are a lot of convenient trading tactics and strategies for day trading.

Characteristics of a Day Trader

Skilled day traders — are traders working for a living rather than as a hobby — are usually well-established in this area. Usually, they have deep knowledge and clear insights into the marketplace as well.

Check out some of the prerequisites for a successful day trader:

Awareness and proper understanding in the marketplace: Individuals who make attempts to day trade without proper knowledge of market background have a risk of losing money. Chart reading and technical analysis is a great skill for a day trader to possess, but without a proper realization of the market you are involved in and the assets that are in that market, charts can be deceptive. Demonstrate your due diligence and make out the particular ins and outs of the goods you buy and sell.

Adequate capital: Day traders seize only risk capital which they can afford themselves to lose. This not only prevents the financial disaster, but it also helps extract stress from their trading. A good deal of capital is often needed to profit effectively from intraday price changes. Access to the margin account is also key, as volatile swings may incur short-term margin calls.

Strategy: The trader needs to have an edge over the rest of the market. There are some various tactics day traders use, including arbitrage, swing trading, and news trading. These strategies are refined until they provide permanent profits and efficiently decrease losses.

Discipline: A lucrative strategy is worthless without discipline. A lot of day traders wind up losing a lot of money because they fail to do business that meets their criteria. Like they claim, "Plan the plan for trade and commerce." Progress is unlikely without discipline.

Day traders count strongly on market volatility in order to make a profit. A stock may be appealing to a day trader if it changes a lot within the day. This could happen because of plenty of different reasons, including earnings report, investor sentiment, corporate news, or even general economic.

Day traders also give preferences to high-liquid stocks because that gives them the chance to amend their position not changing the stock price. If a stock price grows higher, traders can take advantage of buy position. If the price goes down, a trader may solve to short-sell so that he can make a profit when it falls.

Day Trading for a Living

There exist 2 main categories of professional day traders: those who are working on their own and those who are working for a bigger institution.

The major part of day traders who trade for a living work for a bigger institution. These traders benefit from costly analytical software, big numbers of capital and profit, having access to a trading desk, a direct line, and much more. These traders are generally searching for an easy way to make a profit from news events and arbitrage opportunities. Such resources enable them to reap the benefit from these less risky day trades until individual traders can react.

Market participants often trade with their own funds or work with financial support from other people. A limited number of them are open to a trading desk but also have close connections with a brokerage and other services. Nevertheless, the restricted volume of these resources hinders them to compete explicitly with organizational day traders. Instead, they are induced to run more risks. Individual traders typically trade on a day-to-day basis, using technical analysis and swing trades — combined with some leverage — to make adequate profits from such small price movements in highly liquid stocks.

Day trading requires access to some of the most complicated financial services and tools in the marketplace. Day traders typically demand:

Access to a trading desk

This is typically reserved for traders who work for larger companies, or those who run large amounts of money. The trading desk offers immediate executions of orders, which are extremely important for traders when abrupt price changes happen. For instance, when a purchase is announced, day traders looking at merger arbitration may publish their orders before the rest of the market can reap the benefits of the price gap.

Numerous news releases

The news sources with the help of which traders capitalize on, offers more chances for day trading. Traders always must be the first to find out when anything significant occurs. The ordinary dealing room has access to Dow Jones Newswire, permanent coverage of CNBC and other news organizations, and software that continually reviews news releases for important stories.

Analytical software

For many day traders trading software is a must and is very costly. The traders, who rely on technical indicators or swing trades, rely more on software than on news. This software is characterized by the following:

- Genetic and neural applications: Applications that use neural networks and genetic algorithms to improve trading processes are designed to help foresee market shifts in the future.

- Automatic pattern recognition: This means that the trading system detects technical indicators such as channels and flags, or more specific indicators such as Elliott Wave patterns.

- Broker integration: Some of these programs also interact explicitly with the brokerage, allowing for rapid and even automated execution of transactions. This helps to eliminate emotion from trading and improve execution times.

- Back-testing: This helps traders to observe how a policy would have been applied in the past in order to anticipate more precisely how it would be implemented in the future. Bear in mind that previous success is not necessarily representative of potential outcomes.

In combination, these trading instruments give traders an advantage over the rest of the marketplace. It clear that, without them, so many incompetent traders are going bankrupt. As a consequence, certain factors that have an effect on the day traders' earnings prospects are the environment they work in, how much capital they have, and how much time they choose to spend.

The factors complicating the day trading process.

Day trading requires a lot of know-how and practice, and there exist a few factors that can make the trading process complicated.

Firstly, keep in mind that you are running against professional investors whose careers move around trading. Such people are aware of the industry latest technology and changes, and they know how to end up successfully even though they fail. When you get on the bandwagon, it implies that they can get more profits.

Being an individual investor, you are subjected to moral and psychological prejudice. Experienced traders may typically cut these out of their trading strategies but when it concerns your own capital, it seems to be a different story.

Making a decision What and When to Buy

Day traders look for the way to make profits by taking advantage of minute market fluctuations of specific assets (stocks, futures, currencies, and options), typically by using large sums of capital to do so. In determining what to concentrate on — in order, say — a traditional day trader is looking for 3 things:

1. Volatility is solely a function of the anticipated range of market prices — the work environment of a day trader. More volatility implies more income or loss.

2. Liquidity helps you to reach and leave the stock at a reasonable price. Large spreads, for example, or the difference between the product's bid and ask price, and slight slippage, or the variation between the anticipated selling price and the actual price.

3. Trade volume is a measure of how much a stock is purchased and sold within a given time frame —often referred to as the standard daily trading rate. A high level of the volume shows a lot of competition in the stock. The change in the amount of the stock is also a symbol of a price shift, either up or down.

When you have already decided on the type of stock (or other assets) you are searching for, you need to figure out how to define entry points — that's, at what exact moment you are going to make an investment. So, here are trading instruments that will help you to get the idea of how to identify entry points:

- Real-time news platforms: news changes in the market, and it is essential to subscribe to the reliable internet sources that inform you about any possible movements on the market.

- ECN/Level 2 quotes ECN / Level 2 quotes: ECNs or electronic communication systems are computer-based applications displaying the best bid available and requesting quotes from different market participants and then automatically matching and executing orders. Level 2 is a subscription based on a service ensuring real-time access to the Nasdaq order book compiled of price quotes from market makers signing every Nasdaq-listed and OTC Bulletin Board information. Besides, they will give you an idea of the real-time embodiment of instructions.

- Intraday trading candlestick charts: Candlesticks ensure the price activity is rawly analyzed.

If you have a distinct set of entry rules, track additional charts to see if certain conditions are created on a daily basis (suggesting that you are willing to trade on a day trade daily) and more often than not change the price in the expected direction. If so, you'll have a possible entry point for an action plan. You'll then have to decide how to sell or leave those trades.

Choosing the right time when to sell

There are 4 the most common strategies. Let's consider each of them in detail.

1. **Daily pivots.** - Such an approach includes taking advantage of the regular fluctuations of the stock. This is executed by trying to buy at the bottom of the day and sell at the top of the day. Here, the market goal is the next indication of a turnaround.

2. **Scalping.** - Scalping is one of the most prevalent strategies in the trading world. It lies in selling right away after a transaction becomes lucrative. The price target is any figure that translates to "you have cashed in on this deal."

3. **Momentum.** - This strategy is aimed at trading in news releases or trying solid, high-volume trend movements. One kind of momentum trader can trade in news releases and push a pattern before the signs of a turnaround are seen. The other kind of momentum trader will fade the price surge. The price target here is when volume starts to go down.

4. **Fading.** – Fading entails shortening stocks after speedy moves upward. This is focused on the premise that (1) they are over-purchased, (2) early buyers are eager to continue generating money, and (3) current buyers might be terrified. Although it is quite dangerous, this approach may be incredibly rewarding. Here, the price goal is when consumers decide to take steps again.

In most situations, if there is reduced interest in the stock as indicated by level 2 / ECN and quantity, you'll have the opportunity to exit an asset. The profit target should also allow more profit to be made on winning businesses than is lost on losing trades. When your stop-loss is $0.05 away from your entry price, it should be more than $0.05 away from your goal.

Just like your entry point, decide precisely how you are going to exit the markets before you join them. To be repeatable and testable the exit criteria must be reasonably precise.

Swing trading and day trading

Swing trading is a trading method based on fluctuations at the time of a trend formation. In a general sense, this is a set of strategies the main purpose of which is to enter a trend at the time of a pullback (when it is forming) and make a profit. The risk should be minimal. For these reasons, the main features of swing trading are the use of day / week trading periods and clear risk management.

Swing trading can last a little more than a day, or a week.

A trader using this set of strategies is more likely to explore multi-day charts. This is necessary in order to catch higher price movements / fluctuations compared to day trading.

Swing trading concept

One of the main principles of this method is that a swing trader should trade a stock in the direction of a long-term trend, but doing it after the start of mass transactions against this trend. That is, the trader performs transactions on the reversal of the rollback of the stock price, and this is done in relation to the main trend.

Traders usually use the main trends for work. Swing traders should be guided by the following setting: a purchase transaction - at the time of correction (rollback), and profit should be fixed when the movement is canceled in the main trend. The position must be fixed when breaking a line or a support curve.

Of course, the so-called "calm" occurs, when neither bull nor bear trends are observed on the chart. At this time, even indexes can "freeze" on the exchanges but even in this case, there is movement within the channel. This is a pattern that can be predicted. Here, the price will fluctuate between parallel lines. If the trader understands that there is a distinct and fully formed channel in front of him, he can also begin trading in this case, but making the volume of positions smaller. This is necessary, because the risk of loss at the time the trend leaves the "calm" will be higher.

From everything mentioned above, we can make a conclusion that the lowest point that can be reached before the start of the bull trend will be support. In this situation, the trader has two ways: to fix the moment of rollback by taking a long position, not moving away from the support area, or to close positions, waiting for the trend to cancel soon.

Regarding time, the subject trader's interest is long-term stock trends. He is quite capable of holding stocks for days, weeks, and in some cases months, not just hours. This, for the most part, may depend on market sentiment influenced by things like the index price. ▢

The method has some rules have been formulated by more seasoned traders and for the first-time beginners can take advantage of them not to play at their own expense.

For example, a good circumstance for entry can be considered one where the movement is aimed at profit immediately after the start of the transaction. If this is not observed for more than three hours, you should try to close the deal manually as soon as this becomes possible.

The trader should fix immediately, as there is a sharp jump in prices. Then in the future, you can again organize a call at the rollback. It must be remembered that in swing trading, even a small, but quick profit can be of help to continue earning.

Not all transactions should be put off for the next day. The trader needs to close those that are at a loss, prolonging the transaction in profit. Even experienced traders are not advised to open positions at the same time when the market opens or serious trading sessions begin. ⬚

Differences and similarities between day trading and swing trading

The main difference between day and swing trading, is how long the position is held. To a large extent, swing involves transferring an open position to the next day, while day trading should stop before the session closes.

Furthermore, the difference lies in the fact that day traders experience a strong psycho-emotional load associated with the need to change positions at small intervals of 1.3.15 minutes and so on, and they have to monitor their trading to check if they are still then in the field of profit.

Traders who use a day trading strategy, working for themselves or a company, use only this method applying different tools to increase their assets. It is necessary to devote all this time to it, being in stress and tension. Not everyone is able to withstand such a rhythm.

Conversely, trading that applies swing trading usually needs a longer timeframe: the trader holds stocks for days, weeks, and even months. Certainly, the work here is also extremely intense, you need to check the situation constantly and realize whether the situation is favorable, but still the trader has time to in the company of successful traders to exchange experience.

Moreover, there exists quite real opportunity to trade stocks and make for it only part of your time doing other things in parallel.

This makes swing trading attractive for people who want to learn the basics and start earning on the job. For a trader who, for example, works for a third-party company, this can be a step towards independence.

In terms of upfront costs, there are also some differences. Traders who make stock transactions using day trading often have to compete with hedge funds, "high frequency traders" (who work for short periods) and other experienced players, often real professionals.

If a new trader wants to compete with such heavyweights, one needs not only to undergo good training and experience, but, in some cases, to have access to advanced software.

In the case of swing trading, everything is simpler - in order to multiply your assets, a standard computer and ordinary trading tools are suitable. The start in this case is simpler and not fraught with great risks. Therefore, if you want to protect yourself from unnecessary stress, or to prepare yourself for it, it is recommended to start by exploring the possibility of profit on fluctuations.

What strategies can be used when trading on fluctuations

When choosing a strategy for swing trading, you need to take into account the main risks, as in any other trend activity. Remember, that the loss on one transaction should not exceed 2% of all assets, and the ratio of profit to loss should be at least 2: 1.

Analysis and observation are carried out accompanied by additional technical analysis. Most traders consider this approach standard. It will help comprehend which stock or ETF to choose. You can select the technical analysis by yourself; it is significant that they may establish the trend. These are indicators such as, for example, MACD. Goals are priced and set using Fibonacci tools.

Strategy «Modesty»

How to distinguish a beginner from an experienced trader? In most cases, a person who has recently been involved in trade clings to a high profit of 10% -15%. Swinger with great experience sees a future for himself even in such a seemingly insignificant income as 1% - 3%. Very modest, you say? But this is precisely the basis of the proposed strategy. Time is the main resource in swing trading. Therefore, the attention of an experienced player focuses not so much on profit, the process of formation of which can take weeks and months, but on the accumulation of income from a large number of small transactions. Such a strategy can significantly increase the level of total income.

Strategy «Capturing profits on increasing chart»

Initially, no trader knows the time during which the trend will last. For this reason, swing traders try to enter into a bullish deal only after the precise understanding that the trend of the instrument still remains upward. For this, movement is distinguished from the trend. If the price is higher than yesterday's maximum, the trader, after he has conducted a risk analysis and found a "entry point", can enter the deal.

Stop-loss position is calculated by finding the lowest point. When a trader notices that the price is below a point, it is necessary to exit the transaction. Then he finds the profit target, it should be the maximum point of the trend, which recently had a tendency to rise. As soon as it is achieved, it's time to think about the exit, as the trader has already earned.

Strategy-advice "surveillance"

Markets do not remain in the active phase all the time. Quite often there are times when markets are inactive. As a result, traders do not make large profits. We observe minor fluctuations in most cases compared with large trends. The task of swing trading is to learn how to maximize your assets on these extremely minor fluctuations.

Everything happens this way: a swing trader determines the assets or futures from the number of shares that are currently traded most actively from the ETF. Their oscillations should take place in wide channels, which, in turn, must be clearly defined. For convenience, traders usually compile and constantly update the list of stocks present in the ETF. This will simplify trend tracking and allow you to respond on time. You can use Meta Trader 4, and more specifically, the function of creating a separate profile for each ETF. The platform will offer those methods useful for applying in this strategy, trend analysis, for example, chart.

Conclusions about swing trading

This method of trading is sometimes compared with Eastern spiritual practices, as a swing trader must have calm and professionalism that borders on art.

A trader who strives to close only successful transactions has the following skills:

- knowledge of trading theory;

- understanding of trend behavior;

- the study of cycle and price models;

- possession of volumetric methods of analysis.

A swing trader who sincerely dreams of success and asset growth should learn to use the ability to come up with non-standard combinations while trading stocks and feel the market processes well, predict the activity of other traders or companies, anticipate the trend behavior.

It is believed that swing is the most suitable trading style for a trader who has just begun his professional path. This is a good school for understanding the trend. And an experienced trader will find for himself a good potential for earning by trading stocks.

HTF trading

High-Frequency Trading (HFT): what is it and how it affects the market.

High-Frequency Trading (HFT) is a type of algorithmic trading that is distinguished by its high speed, high capital turnover, and short terms of assets possession. For high-frequency trading, robots and powerful computers are used that conclude dozens of transactions in literally milliseconds. Usually, they trade in small volumes to try out the market and often work under the so-called dark pools. Therefore, you will never figure out that a high-frequency trader is against you. HFT traders often stand behind the so-called flash crash - sudden market crashes followed by a rebound.

High-Frequency Exchange Trading

High-frequency trading accounts for more than 70% of all orders on the US stock exchanges, more than 50% of transactions in the Russian stock market, 40% in Europe and 10% in Asia. To provide all the necessary speed for HFT, the exchange must have a server with the possibility of collocation, that is, the trader's server must be in the same data center or cloud as the exchange server.

More and more traders are relying on electronics and automation, and this is happening in all markets. Market makers and arbitrage traders trade more efficiently, which affects pricing, price discovery, and liquidity. Arbitrage windows are getting smaller and they are closing faster, which indicates a more efficient and mature market.

Today, many HFT companies and traders are gradually moving to the cryptocurrency market, because, firstly, it is much more volatile than traditional markets, which makes it possible to earn money, and secondly, cryptocurrency exchanges need HFT companies and liquidity providers. The fact is that in traditional markets, market makers support liquidity and at the moment when it becomes unprofitable to close liquidity holes at their own expense, they attract HFT companies or use high-frequency trading themselves. To put it simply, the cryptocurrency market is a brand-new way to make a profit for traders and companies using high-frequency algorithmic trading.

High-Frequency Cryptocurrency Trading

Algo trading is not news on the cryptocurrency market, but server colocation allows you to take trading to a whole new level. A number of exchanges already offer collocation services - for example, Xena Exchange, Huobi, Gemini, and ErisX. In particular, Huobi representatives have recently said that one of their customers makes about 800,000 transactions per day due to collocation capabilities. This means that the HFT in the crypto is already a reality.

Advantages and disadvantages of HFT trading

Advantages:

1. Increases liquidity

2. Increases trading volume

3. Reduces bid-ask spread

4. Increases Pricing Efficiency

Disadvantages:

*   Enhances volatility

*   HFT traders earn at the expense of small players

*   Sometimes HFT is associated with prohibited manipulations, including spoofing and layering

Spoofing and the so-called layering are automated market manipulation mechanisms that allow you to overtake other market participants. Spoofers create the illusion of high demand or supply of an asset by placing many limit orders on one side of the glass, so it seems that there is pressure on the market to buy or sell. The layering technique lies in the fact that firstly the trader creates and then cancels a large number of orders in order to make the price rise or fall.

High-Frequency Trading Strategies

Usually, HFT traders combine several strategies. Since they never keep an asset for a long time, they constantly have to make decisions about portfolio allocation. For this, algorithmic models are used, the success of which depends on the ability to process large amounts of data. High-frequency trading algorithms are a combination of several arbitrage strategies that are implemented at tremendous speed, plus market-making.

Types of HFT Strategies

- HFT Execution Strategy

- Order Flow Forecasting Strategies

- Automatic HFT Arbitration

- HFT Market Making Strategy

HFT strategy execution: constitutes an implementation of large orders of institutional investors with zero or minimal influence on the price. This includes trading at an average price, weighted by volume (VWAP), allowing you to close orders at a price better than the average market, as well as trading at an average price, weighted by time (TWAP), with which you can buy and sell assets without affecting the price market.

Order Flow Forecasting Strategies: a trader tries to anticipate the placing of orders by large players, to be the first to open positions and profit from a price change caused by a large transaction.

Automatic HFT Arbitration - the trader makes a small profit when there is a variance in price for the same instrument.

HFT Market Making Strategy is necessary in order to set a quote (the last price at which a transaction was made with an asset) and constantly update it.

High-Frequency Trading Software

There are two main ways to join the ranks of HFT traders. The first is to find a specialized broker. The second is to buy powerful equipment and install special software. Several developers are represented on the market, but before you pay serious money for the program, you need to plan your next actions.

1. You will need to decide on strategies. A software developer will sell you only the program itself - without a strategy, algorithm, or signals.

2. HFT trading is associated with high costs: this includes expenses for colocation, broadband Internet, payment for broker services, etc.

3. High-frequency trading programs require careful tuning before trading.

High-frequency trading is gaining popularity in the market

HFT is an extremely effective way to trade, that's why it is the name of the game in financial markets. Institutional investors spend billions of dollars annually on the development and implementation of high-frequency strategies. HFT is conquering the new markets - including the cryptocurrency market - and is increasingly publicized in the media. Ordinary traders can only accept the presence of HFT and, if possible, avoid the traps of high-frequency traders.

Day trading tools

What are the trading tools?

A day trading tool is everything that was applied in order to make a profit from trading.

Some tools are tangible. However, the most important of them are intangible and constantly evolving. Day trading is a serious business. The day trading requires specific tools and skills to produce the best results.

Some trading instruments cost money, some of them are free and need more time to capitalize on them.

Think of trade as a business. Compared to other companies, overhead and variable costs are low. Costs are also anticipated by applying proper planning.

Make sure you have these 13 basic tools to speed up your trading success.

- **Designed trading plan:** The developed trading plan is the most frequently disregarded aspect of day-to-day trading is the designed trading plan. It is a really simple oversight to make. The best trading strategies involve flexibility for the individual trader. This ensures that they are not sold on the mass. Everyone is attempting to offer you a "one size fits all" approach, but the standardized strategy isn't the one that can bring you where you want to go.

- **High-speed internet:** Online internet access is a vital part of trading. If you don't show to the market your desire to trade, trading will stop.

Well, it sounds elementary but secure and effective internet access is a must for a committed day trader. It's costly not to be capable of doing your job.

Minimizing the risk of a power outage is a significant perk. Getting a backup service and the correct equipment is a simple protection policy.

- **Online broker:** Until you have a seat in the market or have a defined deal with a financial company, you will use the services of a broker.

Define your desirable market and trading goods in your trading plan. Then apply the knowledge and skills to select a broker that can ensure access to them for you.

The right broker for the trading transaction is not the cheapest one. Low prices also attach extra expenses to your trading.

On the other side, high-priced brokers do not always cost extra money. You should pay special attention to what you get from your broker for the money you pay.

Look for a broker to meet your trading strategy demands. Make sure you established a backup broker or even two as you get more serious about your day trading.

- **Trading platform:** A lot of brokers come up with their own proprietary trading platform. This platform is a software used to enter orders. Many of them also ensure you to analyze data to make trading decisions.

On the other hand, there are several multi-broker or broker-independent trading platforms offering a high-quality service. These dedicated tools make trading across multiple brokerages possible via a single software interface.

There are several pros of a multi-broker platform. These include there is no need in learning a new platform if your broker decided to quit the business. They are also useful if you consider your needs to be served better by another brokerage and solve to toggle.

Broker independent multi-broker platforms are also narrow-focused. They are dealing with creating a perfect platform and focus on that.

- **Data feed:** Trading platforms ought to provide a data feed. Some trading platforms provide a free data feed free of charge, whereas others do not. Data appears in the form of historical and real-time trading volumes and price, as well as news feeds.

Whatever data channel you pick, make sure it ensures the right products and markets for you. You have an option to select what you wish and customize things the way you like.

- **High-speed computer:** This is one of the more controversial requirements in the trading. The accessibility of platforms having mobile interface opportunities also triggers this discussion. However, the discussion ends when it comes to da trading. Those people who are focused on their results seriously should have a fast computer.

- **Capital:** There are a number of businesses where the creativity and the strategy are what you need. You could be a stock day trader that fits the pattern day trader demands, or you could be a futures trader that meets the margin demand. Trading requires money, no matter what the situation is on the market. Save up funds and make your trading way easier.

- **Education:** The sole right secure weapon tool in the trading market are education and training.

Neglecting this tool is the main reason of many trading stories about failure. Doctors, lawyers, Starbucks baristas – everybody needs education and training to succeed.

Some education and training programs and courses are beyond the means. The expense is always tiny in comparison to the losses that can save you from taking. Large losses almost always are materialized through inexperience and ignorance.

If you are sure to have funds for trading, invest them wisely and first and foremost deposit them into your brain. Your future self will be grateful.

- **Practice:** Only everyday practice will help to improve your trading quickly. You will find out which techniques work for you and the ones you should avoid.

Trying out the strategy for yourself is the only way to choose the best one. Test the method. More to the point, test the strategy and method the way you like to trade.

Don't be in a rush to do anything that's not suitable for you. Start acquiring your trading experience with a simulator. Follow it up with the proper steps to push that strategy to effective trading.

- **Strategy:** The number of different trading strategies is as diversified as those of traders who deploy them.

A lot of traders are faced with difficulties because the option is immense. They also alter their approach after a brief amount of time, depending on what they observe on the horizon. They assume that all modern developments work better than their plan of action.

This is a bad tendency. Stick to one or two great, powerful strategies and allow them more time to work.

Strategies require time to demonstrate permanent and conducive results. Begin with fewer trading strategies and you can succeed with them free of interference. Add or delete your policy chart as your trading abilities and outcomes determine.

- **Specific tools:** Strategies during the day trading platform differ a lot. Even the tools for deploying the various strategies are quite specific.

For instance:

1. High-quality news sources support a policy that exchanges data and earnings reports. Yet the same news stream may be a waste of time for an investor struggling with chart trends.

2. High accuracy of historical databases and back-testing engines can be powerful. They are a great tool for traders who use 100% automatic systems. The same methods will not be suitable for traders with a flexible system.

3. Patented indicators are a convenient expense for bright traders. These traders rape the benefit and create a secure business case for the expense. Similar indicators are of a less value to a trader who can't incorporate the trading instrument into his trading plan.

Consolidate your trading operations. Make sure you that you have the finest trading instruments, but only for the strategies you are currently trading. There is no need to seize every tool out there.

Big-time traders know the ropes of a trading world. This also means that they have chosen specialized tools for their attention. Make sure you choose the arsenal of tools that best suits your own strategies.

- **Discipline:** It is impossible to find it on a store shelf. It doesn't exist online and it is not the feature we are born with.

Discipline. It is one of the most significant features an intelligent trader must possess.

Discipline in trading may appear in the form of studying and exercising practice. It can take at least 30 minutes per day and success is guaranteed.

Consistency is the hallmark of discipline and the pledge of successful trading.

- **Obligation:** Long-term obligations can be subtle. Trading is a challenge, and mastering true trading is a real mastery that takes years. A strong obligation is an intangible instrument. It keeps traders following their discipline over the long run.

There is always a way for the committed. In the markets, you can find the success you want.

Keep in mind that overnight successes happen rarely. Long-lived overnight successes don't exist. Commit to trading.

Apply these 13-day trading tools to achieve maximum results. This is a perfect way to make the most of your time spent on trading.

Opening a brokerage account

A brokerage account is a kind of online account opened by traders for investing. It allows buying securities and saving for retirement more easily. Opening a brokerage account is the very step before you are going to invest in the stock market or trading forex. If you still haven't got a clue of how to open your first brokerage account then familiarize yourself with step-by-step instructions on how to top up your future account and select the finest possible account type you need.

Step 1. Choose a broker

The broker is an intermediary between an individual and the exchange. It provides access to stock trading. When choosing a broker to open an account, be guided by the following recommendations:

- Carefully read the terms of a particular intermediary.

- Assess whether he suits you based on your own financial capabilities (minimum deposit amount, fees, commissions, additional services) and objectives pursued (how often do you plan to conclude transactions, do you need access to foreign exchange markets, etc.).

- Check for a license. In the absence of the license, the broker activity is illegal,

ATTENTION! If a license is available, then it will be freely available on the official resource of the intermediary, but it can be faked to attract customers. Therefore, check the broker according to a single list of financial market participants.

- Rate the credibility rating of the broker. You can check it on the official website of the intermediary and the resources of rating agencies.

- Examine his reputation, read other customers' reviews.

- Learn about the broker's experience and the scope of his activities. Dealing with novice intermediaries is cheaper, but riskier.

Promotional promises of brokerage companies - this is not the benchmark to rely on making the final choice. However, if you are promised a specific and guaranteed income, then bear in mind, that this is an advertising trick, because it is impossible to accurately predict the result on the exchange. The best brokerage companies do not try to mislead the client and guarantee him the provision of services at a high level.

Step 2. Determine the type of brokerage account

Traders can open brokerage accounts using different ways: as a margin account or as a cash account. However, if you open a margin account, you must open a cash account as well. Also, you can open individual accounts to save up for retirement. Although, retirement accounts have more limits, your trading options are more restricted in those accounts.

Margin accounts

There is no need to have as much money on hand to buy stocks when you are going to open a margin account. Such type of account enables you to borrow certain amounts of money using securities or cash existing in the account as collateral. Each respectable brokerage company has its own screening process to define whether it is possible to make purchases on margin.

The Federal Reserve needs a minimum investment of $2,000 to establish a margin account and generally restricts the sum you may borrow on a margin to 50 % of the original purchasing price. Not all stocks should be bought on the margin. When you buy the stock at a margin, you pay interest rates on margin loans, but the major part of brokerage companies charges comparatively low rates to promote transaction business.

Before opening a margin account, the company usually wants you to sign the hypothecation agreement which lays the guidelines regarding the transaction and enables the broker to provide access to the account if the balance of the account falls below the required maintenance margin. The deal also allows the broker to lend the stock to short-sellers.

Cash accounts

The typical brokerage account is a cash account, well-known as a Form 1 account. With the help of a cash account, you have to pay the entire cost of any purchases before the date of the transaction settlement.

Currently, very few brokers provide you with that kind of flexibility. Many brokers demand funds to buy stocks to be in your cash account before you can make an order. The amount of cash to present on deposit is varied by a broker.

IRAs and other retirement accounts

IRAs and other accounts you are saving up for retirement sometimes enable you to trade options, but margin trading is forbidden. Such restrictions serve for your protection in order to avert dangerous losses in your long-term investments which never should be placed under such a high level of danger. The amount can be contributed annually to all retirement accounts restricted by the Internal Revenue Code.

Although you will manage to find a brokerage company allowing to trade by using options — puts and calls, that is a kind of option —nevertheless, you take risk penalties for defined trading activities that take place in your retirement account whenever the IRS defines the account is being used for trading goals, not for long-term investing.

Step 3. Choose a tariff plan

In order to understand which broker tariff plan is the best for you, you should decide on the main strategy on the exchange: an active trader or a passive investor.

If you are not going to make deals constantly, but fund your investment portfolio with small amount of money 1-2 times a month, then for you, first of all, it is not the transaction fee that matters, but the payment of the depository (the service where the securities are stored), which can be fixed monthly.

For an active trader, who makes transactions daily on the stock exchange, the commission amount for one operation matters. In this case, you need to choose a tariff with a minimum transaction fee. The monthly payment of the depository in this situation does not matter much.

Step 4. Choose the method of opening a brokerage account (online or in the office)

Almost any brokerage company offers 2 ways to open a brokerage account: in the office or online.

If you have decided to open a brokerage account in the office, you only need to collect the necessary package of documents, the rest of the work will be executed by company employees.

You can open an account via the Internet without leaving your home, but there are certain subtleties in this matter:

- On the broker's official website, you must choose the option "open an account" function, enter personal data and information for feedback (e-mail, phone), and then indicate the type of account and the tariff plan.

  Usually, detailed information regarding tariffs is contained on the site itself - you only need to study it carefully. If you can't make the choice yourself, you can ask for a consultation with a specialist.

- After filling in the data and confirming it using a code from SMS, you must identify yourself through the broker's website. If you already have an account there, you only need to log in and provide access to your data.

- If the identification was successful, you conclude a contract using a simple electronic signature.

- Next, you will need to enter your payment information, fill out a questionnaire, provide a scanned copy of your passport, and complete the registration.

The main danger when opening an online account is the risk of getting into a trap to a scam site. Therefore, if the site seems suspicious to you and you are not sure that this is the official resource of the company, do not rush to enter your data.

Step 5. Get the necessary documents for opening a brokerage account ready.

The package of documents for opening a brokerage account may vary slightly among different companies, but the basic documents that you will need are as follows:

- Questionnaire and application form of the sample established in the company;

- Passport, driving license (or other identification document confirming the person who is opening an account)

- Other documents your company ask for.

Step 6. Get confirmation of opening a brokerage account

After providing all the documents and signing the contract, the data will be sent to the exchange to register your account. This may take up to 48 hours, after which you will get access to the exchange, and SMS will be sent to the indicated number confirming the opening of a brokerage account.

Step 7. Top up your account.

You can top up your account at any convenient time. Until this moment it will be inactive. You can fund a brokerage account by:

- transferring from your bank card

- transferring from your savings account

- cash through the broker's cash desk in his office

So, after the successful opening and funding of your brokerage account, you can buy stocks, bonds, currency on the exchange. Applying a reasonable approach to investing in the exchange, your capital will grow and soon you will make bundles.

How to choose the right stocks for trading?

Stocks are perhaps the most common investment tool on the market. They are suitable for both beginners and professional investors. Let's figure out how to choose and buy suitable stocks.

Choose the scope of the company

The choice of the industry should be based on your interests and experience. For example, if you get the hang of interiors, pay attention to manufacturers of furniture and household goods. If you are into computer games - take a closer look at game developers and video card manufacturers. It is better to choose not one industry, but several, as you will need to distribute your investments. You will be better versed in companies that affect your personal or professional interests.

Explore companies in the chosen field

Compare companies of the same industry: maybe right now dark horses demonstrate better results than recognized industry leaders. To do this, go to the website of the exchange you are interested in (MICEX, NYSE or NASDAQ) and get acquainted with the list of traded assets.

Of course, to become a shareholder of a large company - this sounds good and more reliable. However, it is also impossible to deprive the attention of second-tier players, since their shares can rise at any time. Such ups can make shareholders wealthy. Make a list of companies that you find interesting. Each of them needs to be thoroughly studied.

Look through the company profile

Work through all the available information about the company. How has it developed? How was it transformed? How did important events in the company's life in the past affect the movement of its shares? What are the plans for the future? Quite often, the vector of the company's movement in the past determines its future development. Pay special attention to profit and loss statements.

Pay attention not only to achievements but also to serious failures. It is important to understand how the company copes with difficulties and what happens to its shares at this moment. This will help assess your risks at the start. Do not forget about liquidity: the company and what it produces should be liquid, both now and in the future.

Learn Company News

The company's plans directly affect your income from investing in it. If the company plans to release a new product, if it has made a discovery, it can play into your hands. Everything brand new generates interest and, therefore, increases the likelihood of rising stock prices, although it is not a guarantee of quick returns. For example, a change of leadership can both positively and negatively affect the business of the company, and hence its value. Do not also think that companies always grow rapidly. Shares of many heavyweight corporations are growing slowly, but confidently.

Explore company and industry dynamics

Evaluate the dynamics of the company and the industry where it operates over the past few years. If the growth rate is falling or even worse negative, then looking in this direction doesn't worth it. Buying stocks after a period of sharp growth is like jumping into the last car of a running train.

The dynamics of such enterprises is generally healthier and more predictable, and predictability always reduces risks. Based on financial reports, predict its future and evaluate whether you are ready to be a shareholder of the company with such a future. Probable negative events should also not be forgotten, this will help to assess the risks soberly and your attitude to them.

Read analytics

If you have not skipped the previous points, then you have already conducted some analysis. Now you can address the opinion of professionals, and see what they think about the prospects of the companies you have chosen. Large investment banks regularly publish their own recommendations. The opinions of prominent experts and professional investors can be found on the Internet (including on their personal pages on social networks). Of course, analysts are not psychics, and they cannot predict the exact scenario. However, a professional view from the outside can open your eyes to the missing details. In addition, professional analysts often possess insider information. You can study analytics in previous years. This will help assess whether past forecasts have come true.

Build a Stock Portfolio

Some of the companies from the initial list are eliminated during the detailed review of the previous paragraphs. Some of them are in economic decline, some are already at the peak of their prosperity, etc. As a result, you will have a list of one, two or more market players. The stocks of a company having bigger prospects according to analysis carried out before, should be bought. It is not necessary to dwell on one company from a field of activity. You can invest in the shares of two or three competitive enterprises, and only then monitor whose performance will be better.

Try to have the stocks of 10-12 companies in your portfolio so that a possible drop in one asset is offset by others. As we mentioned earlier, you need to invest in different areas of activity.

Investing in stocks and making profit out of them is not complicated, and do not be confused by the multi-stage process. In this case, multi-stage does not likely complicate the process, but facilitates i and improves the result. A rational approach takes time and your attention: warned means armed, and with stocks. The main thing to remember is that you spend your time and effort on minimizing risks and generating income, and this stimulates.

10 The Most Common Market Strategies

Day trading is the process carried out on the market aimed at buying and selling financial tools within a day. If the trading is carried out properly then taking advantage of small price movements can be a lucrative business. On the contrary, it can be a quite risky game for beginners or traders who don't stick to a well-thought-out strategy.

However, not all brokers are suitable for the high volume of trades that are carried out by day traders. Still, there are some brokers elaborated with taking into consideration the day trader.

Let's look into the underlying day trading principles and then carry on choosing the perfect time when to buy and sell, pervasive day trading strategies, basic charts principal patterns, and how to avoid losses.

Day Trading Strategies

1. Awareness Is Power.

Being aware of principal trading processes is not enough. Day traders also need to monitor and keep pace with the latest events and news on the stock market taking into account the economic outlook, rate plans and the Fed's interest.

So, accomplish your home task. Draw up a bucket list of the stocks you would like to trade and be always kept in the loop of the general markets and selected companies. Keep track of business news and look for reliable financial sources.

2. Put Aside Funds

Estimate how much money you want to roll the dice for each trade. A number of day-to-day traders lose less than 1% to 2% in their trading accounts. For instance, if you hold a $40,000 trading portfolio and choose to lose 0.5 percent of your money for each deal, the potential exchange loss is $200 (0.5 percent * $40,000).

The surplus amount of financial resources should be set aside in order to trade. You should always be ready to lose them. Bear in mind, it may or may not happen.

3. Put Aside Time, as well.

Day trading takes your free time so that's why the name of it is day trading. In fact, you will have to spend the main part of your day on it. Don't even look at it if you are restricted in time.

The trading procedure needs a trader permanently to keep track of the current situation on the market and to estimate spot opportunities, which can jump at any time within trading hours. On-the-spot decisions are the key.

4. Get started with small

As a novice trader, concentrate on a maximum of 1-2 stocks in the course of a session. Monitoring and looking for opportunities are more easily with a few stocks. Nowadays, it is extremely pervasive to know how to trade with fractional shares, so you can clarify specific, smaller dollar amounts you want to invest.

5.   Avert Penny Stocks

Probably you are hunting for transactions and low prices but still staying away from penny stocks. Frequently, these stocks are illiquid, and the chance to hit a jackpot is bleak.

Most of the stocks, priced under $5 per share, are de-listed from the major stock markets and may only be exchanged over-the-counter (OTC). Keep clear of these until you have a particular chance to do your work.

6.   Time Those Trades

When investors and traders place the orders, they start to implement as soon as the markets open up in the morning, that leads to the volatility of a price. An experienced player can make an adequate choice and recognize patterns to make profits. However, it can be better for beginners to read the market without making any moves for the first 15 to 20 minutes.

As a rule, the middle hours are less fragile. As a result, dynamics toward the closing bell starts to go up again. Although the rush hours ensure opportunities, it's safer for newbies to avert them for the first time.

7. Reduce Losses with Limited Orders

Solve what kind of orders you are going to use in order to enter and exit trading. Are you going to use limit orders or market orders? When you post a market order, it is implemented at the most reasonable price accessible at this time—therefore, the price is guaranteed.

Meanwhile, a restricted order, ensures the price but not the implementation. The limited orders help you trade more accurately, wherein you quote your price (not unrealistic but executable) for buying and selling as well. More seasoned day traders may use options strategies to protect their positions too.

8. Be down-to-earth concerning profit

In order to be lucrative a strategy doesn't need to win all the time. A lot of traders only benefit 50-60% from their total trades. Make sure that the risk for each trade is limited to a specific percentage of the account, and that methods of entry and exit are determined and taken down distinctly.

9.   Keep calm.

There are occasions when the stock market tries out your nerves. In the capacity of a day trader, you need to master the skills of keeping fear, greed and hope, at bay. Your decisions should be soberly ruled by common sense but not emotions.

10.   Adhere to the Plan

Seasoned traders have to act quickly, but not to think for a long time. Why? Because they have a designed trading strategy beforehand, alongside the discipline to adhere to that strategy. Following your formula closely rather than trying to pursue the profits is also of a great importance. Don't let your feelings and emotions run over you, and set your plan aside. Among day traders, there's a catch phrase: "Plan your trade and trade your plan."

Let's consider some of the reasons why day trading can be so complicated before we dive into some of the ins and outs of day trading.

Investment Management

Functions, tasks, and stages of investment management

Investment management constitutes a combination of methods, techniques, and principles allowing you to manage the investment processes and financial resources flow effectively in order to obtain a stable income. It acts as an integral part of the overall management.

Management activity is directly related to investment processes and carried out at several hierarchical levels. If we recall the microeconomics and macroeconomics, then we can easily enumerate them. It is about states, constituent entities, municipalities, and individual enterprises.

It is quite natural that at each of the listed levels, investment activity has its own specifics and characteristics. However, this management, regardless of where it is carried out, based on the same principles and methods, and also solves similar problems.

Main functions

Investment management has three main functions:

- planning;

- organizational;

- coordinating.

The planning function of management refers to the initial stage of the investment process. It characterizes the competent development of the only right strategy for investing funds. Here is the formation of an investment policy. Without its implementation, it is impossible to build the enterprise, municipality, or country activities properly; make it reliable enough and sustainable in the long run.

The organizational function of management refers to the stage of direct construction of an investment project. Here, investors should decide on many important issues, in the absence of which, the further implementation of the developed strategy and policy of the investee would be just impossible. In particular, it is about identifying the needs for raising funds out of external sources, finding a strategic partner and investor, choosing investment tools, forming an investment portfolio, and other events.

At the same time, the investment activity of an economic entity should be at the level that corresponds to the chosen development strategy of the company the best.

The coordinating function of management refers to the stage of direct implementation of a developed and agreed project. Investment managers must constantly monitor and coordinate all actions and activities aimed at achieving their goals. In the case of the identified violations and shortcomings, specific decisions should be made to amend the project enabling to neutralize and compensate for the shortcomings.

Existing goals and objectives

Investment management should perform the following tasks:

- ensure the production growth and economic indicators of the company;

- maximize the profitability of all investment objects; minimize the risks that always accompany the activities of the investor. The principal objective of such management can be considered the selection of investment assets that are optimal for the current economic situation. They should combine the highest possible profitability and the lowest risk level.

Thus, you can consider investment management to be a set of measures aimed at preserving and increasing the capital of an enterprise or company.

Main stages

Investment management can be divided into several successive stages:

- tactics development;

- securities analysis;

- investment portfolio formation;

- current portfolio adjustment;

- analytical work on ongoing projects.

Tactics should be developed by considering all the objectives that the investor plans to achieve with this investment. The financial capabilities of the investor, the level of expected return on investment, and the existing level of risk have to be taken into consideration either. You can use 2 types of analysis: technical and fundamental in order to determine the effectivity of the project.

The technical analysis involves constant monitoring of the stock market, as well as forecasting the dynamics of prices for individual assets. The main objective of such an analysis is the timely determination of the growth trend in the value of an asset.

Fundamental analysis provides an introduction to macroeconomic indicators. In order to determine the actual risk level and the expected profitability degree of an investment project, it is necessary to take into account:

- financial stability of the company;

- asset liquidity;

- reputation

Based on such indicators, the investor can determine the prospects for the long-term development of the enterprise. Based on this information, a final decision should be made regarding investments.

Investment managers

All the functions and tasks stated above must be implemented by someone. For this, there is a specialty -

investment manager. Sch employees have a serious responsibility in a company that is actively engaged in investment. Their competencies are to solve numerous problems:

- ensuring the activities of the enterprise in terms of investment;

- tactics and investment strategies determination;

- cash investment policy development;

- drawing up business plans for investment projects;

- ensuring risk reduction and increasing investment profitability;

- analysis of the current financial condition of the business entity;

- the determination of quantitative and qualitative characteristics of securities;

- investment portfolio optimization;

- investment adjustment (if necessary)

- forecasting and assessing the assets;

- monitoring the evaluation of the effectiveness of the ongoing project;

- general regulation of the investment process.

Such kind of managers should be specialists in their field. They have to be aware of the theoretical and practical part of the investment process, possess the skills of mathematical analysis and modeling, be aware of the latest changes in industry legislation. Only in this case, the level of investment management in the company will meet the stringent requirements of work in a period of instability and the global economic crisis.

The average income of a day trader

Trading is a buying and selling on financial exchanges, that is, traders make their profit on the account of successful deals. The average income of a day trader depends on many factors and his personal experience and skills. The trader's salary is the sum of all financial transactions, therefore, even a downside is possible. However, the average earnings of a day trader who is not a beginner and professionally works on financial exchanges is quite high.

What determines the earnings of a trader?

The income of traders always depends on several conditions. These conditions can be divided into several groups:

- The general market condition and financial market situation, that is, under certain failures or rises, traders get a significant profit. At the same time, at these moments some of the traders lose their investments;

- The strategy type and the presence of experience. This category includes both the ability of a trader to calculate the situation and analyze the possibility of profit during the jumps in quotes and his ability to cope with emotions and follow a calculated course

- The amount of invested capital or deposit sum of money. The larger amounts a day trader trades, the greater his actual profit.

If a trader trades consistently without sharp disruptions and applying an effective strategy, then his monthly deposit growth will be approximately 30-40%.

It should be borne in mind that it is impossible to calculate the exact monthly earnings, since taking into consideration all factors that influence the market, each month gives a different profit. In monetary terms, people having higher or special education can earn as much as the average trader earns.

Features influencing the profit of the average trader

The real income of traders who make transactions on binary options or forex is slightly lower. This is due to several features:

- In the stock market, a broader transaction process can be carried out, as there are many more assets.

- The long-term market is more stable than the short-term, which allows suffering fewer losses (at reasonable rates)

- A wider range of tools and strategies allowing to trade with lower risk and get a more stable income;

- A significant advantage of a stock market that, closing the deal here is much easier than in other financial markets.

Besides, real income with a large deposit and high rates will be higher than several plus transactions with a small deposit.

So, what is the percent of various traders' profit in different markets:

- The profit of traders trading on binary options can reach 100% per month, but the total positive income will still not be very high since deposit amounts are an order of magnitude smaller and the risk higher;

- Forex trading depends on the choice of trading assets, but most often the monthly profit does not exceed 50% of the invested funds;

- In perfect circumstances, with all the positive conditions, the trader can make a profit of up to 50% of the invested funds, but it is worth remembering that this case is very rare. Normal profit is about 30% in successful and stable trading.

The successful trending requires a proper approach to trading and the time spent on studying all the day trading features as well. Most truly successful traders do not engage in ill-considered investments. In addition, they have a financial education and treat trading as a job.

The Risk and the Opportunity to Lose Invested Assets

The risk begins before the trader starts trading. If a bad broker was chosen then there is a likelihood of a scam. That is why the choice of a good platform and a licensed broker is the key to successful trading.

The second step is a properly chosen strategy that should function under the condition that the profit will be higher than the loss.

The main feature of the risk is the volatility of the market, so even the best and most seasoned trader can make only a few thousand profits per year. For this reason, you can't become a trader from scratch. This will require start-up capital, which can be invested according to the strategy. This allows you to get a stable income.

The profit of a trader depends on his skills and abilities, but the invested sum of money affects the net profit most of all. If there is no good start-up capital, then the income of the trader will be insignificant. These traders are already trading with a very large starting deposit, and that's why their income is a stable income of 10 thousand dollars per month.

Trading Psychology

Trading Psychology relates to emotional state and feelings that help regulate success or failure in trading securities. Trading psychology reflects many facets and behavior of the trader affecting his trading actions. Trading psychology can be as significant as other qualities such as awareness, skills and experience and in defining trading success.

The perfectionism, egocentrism, self-confidence are the most important facets that drive trading behavior.

Comprehension of trading psychology

Trading psychology may be correlated with a few common feelings and actions that are often market-trade catalysts.

Conventional market-driven activity characterizations attribute the most emotional trading to either perfectionism or egocentrism.

Perfectionism

Perfectionism often causes the feeling of pain due to the loss and drowns out the pleasure of victory. Desperately trying to feel "good," perfectionists often rely on unrealistic high ideals. They think that they will finally find the necessary state of satisfaction if they simply reach a certain point X (many things can be substituted for point X, including appearance, wealth, popularity or achievements). Since point X is an unattainable goal, perfectionists use their ideals as the basis for self-criticism when they cannot achieve the level of efficiency they need.

The keynote of the perfectionist's emotional state is the phrase "I'm not good enough." Perfectionists are forced to work more and more, because they never feel competent enough, worthy and best. Thus, even when the perfectionist makes a profit from the transaction, he will always focus on that part of the market movement that he missed. When the trade does not go well, he seeks various reasons to reproach himself for some mistakes. achieving success, but all they do, in fact, is a breakdown of confidence. By focusing on efficiency that is inappropriate to ideals, perfectionists consciously transform successes into defeats, losses into failures. They try to justify their perfectionism by striving for success, but all they do is the undermining of confidence.

Perfectionism is manifested as an internal dialogue of a negative nature and constant self-accusation. It can be recognized in the form of frustration and anger when trading does not bring the desired results. The perfectionist's inner conversation resembles self-flagellation. In order to defeat the signs of perfectionism in yourself, you need to make an effort and try to establish an internal dialogue and translate it into a positive channel. Mentally talk to yourself as a close friend. Most people treat others with respect and love, but have not learned how to treat themselves the same way. If you relate to friends with a greater understanding than to yourself in the same situation, then you are not a friend to yourself.

If something goes wrong in the trade, the constructive trader will ask himself the question "What lesson can I learn from this situation?" Rather than

"What happened to me?" The best antidote to perfectionism is the ability to reassure oneself: "Better deals in the future." It's important not to miss out on these best deals while you engage in self-criticism!

Ego

Everyone loves to win in the market. It is natural to be proud of the fact that you closed the day with a profit, since you received a reward for your efforts. However, when a bloated ego is involved in the trading process, things go much further. If the transactions are profitable, the trader is proud of himself, but as soon as the account enters the drawdown, an emotional decline occurs. This has a tremendous impact on trade over time. In fact, the trader sends psychological weapons in his direction, ready to fire at any moment, as soon as the market analysis fails.

Most traders are aware of the dangers of using high leverage. A trader who is accustomed to trading 2 lots on the S&P 500 with a tick value of $ 25 will be extremely uncomfortable conducting 100-lot trading operations, as each minimum price change becomes equal to $ 1250. At such high rates, trading in a psychological sense will be completely different. It will be difficult for such a trader to manage positions.

By investing your emotions in trading, you work with the maximum psychological leverage. In the currency of self-esteem, you trade 100 lots. Thus, most of your emotional score is spent on every transaction, which inevitably affects your decisions about reducing losses, timely entry and exit. A successful trader focuses on the quality of the transaction, and a selfish trader on their profitability.

Selfishness has a devastating effect on the trader and often forces him to make unreasonable transactions only in order to win back recent losses. The constant emotional roller coaster caused by a series of winning / losing trades is equally a consequence of the ego involved in the trade. We already know that the perfectionism of traders is given out by such emotions as anger and disappointment. The manifestation of selfishness can be identified by symptoms such as euphoria and depression. Therefore, if trading makes you depressed, you need to think about it, because the reason for this is not just a fluctuation in equity.

So, what is an effective way to get rid of selfishness in trading? Direct your self-esteem to other areas of life: recreational interests, non-trading activities, personal relationships and spiritual life. Often, we form our self-esteem solely on the basis of trading results, only because other facets of our lives are not properly developed. A balanced life promotes a balanced trade.

Self-confidence

Typically, traders complain about the lack of confidence in trading, but very often they are just the same hampered by excessive self-confidence. It stems from a lack of understanding of the complexity of markets and underestimation of the challenges associated with them. Self-confident traders are not serious about the market. They believe that a couple of setups from the next trading book or the purchase of a modern trading platform will help them consistently earn money in the market.

Such traders do not want to gradually move to success. They oppose the idea that screen time is the best teacher. Instead of starting trading with one contract and waiting for the trading results to stabilize, self-confident traders want to operate with large positions and make a profit here and now. Unreasonable and excessive self-confidence forces such traders to make impulsive decisions. Instead of waiting until the setup is fully formed, they enter the transaction prematurely. Self-confident traders do not wait for the approval of short-term and long-term models and take all transactions, thereby working to enrich brokers.

A distinctive feature of self-confident traders is that they trade excessively actively, and do not wait for the appropriate opportunity that the market provides them with. Setting goals for profit for every day or week is one of the manifestations of self-confidence. Traders who trade consciously know that market volatility is constantly changing and there are times when there is simply no opportunity to enter a position. However, a confident trader believes that the market is subject to him.

Emotional signs of self-confidence are impatience and impulsiveness. Self-confident traders usually over-trade. They are more afraid to miss the opportunity to open another deal than to lose money. The main means of self-confidence is trading based on strict rules verified on a demo account (or on a real one with opening small positions). Strict adherence to the rules will allow the trader to get rid of impulsiveness in making trading decisions.

Trading consciously, a complex conscious process wedges itself between the impulse and the action. The action is preceded by an awareness of its motives and consideration of the consequences. This approach to trading helps traders make effective trading decisions.

It is clear that the defects described above are not completely independent of each other. Often these defects are manifested in a complex. For example, a trader can open a position because of self-confidence, and then hold it for too long because of the stubbornness and pride associated with the ego. Regardless of the trader's flaw: perfectionism, ego or self-confidence, the main problem is the same - trading with a focus on oneself and not on the market.

If you think about yourself (that is, how much you will earn or lose, how well or poorly you trade, how successful or unfortunate you are, how much better you could trade), then you will not be able to focus well on the market. It's not about you. The point is the ability to interpret stock information correctly and make effective decisions. In order to learn how to do it qualitatively, it is necessary to completely immerse yourself in the process of "reading" the market, become one with it, feel it, and not just watch it. You cannot correctly interpret the market, lost in feelings of anger, disappointment, delight, guilt, depression or impatience.

The most serious vice in trading is the tendency to take everything into a personal account and focus on the result of trading, losing sight of the process itself. If you sufficiently express yourself outside of trading, develop physically, socially, spiritually and professionally, you will find that the market is no longer a place for you to increase your self-esteem. This approach to life will allow you to get rid of the destructive influence of emotions on your trade.

10 Golden Rules for Successful Trading

Trading is more of an art than a science. Therefore, it is impossible to foresee all the failures that may arise in the trading process. It is unrealistic to draw up universal requirements for all occasions. However, it's still necessary to have some kind of "lighthouses", landmarks that will not allow you to go astray while sailing on rough seas. Therefore, you can try to formulate some rules that you always want to follow. There are ten such rules.

1. Limit your losses

It is extremely important to limit your losses for each position strictly: that is, already entering the market, you must clearly realize at what level you will fix the loss if the price goes against you. It happens that straight away after such a loss fix, the market turns around and goes in your direction - but without you. However, this can only motivate you to better define exit points - but by no means to refuse to use "stop-loss" in principle. Bear in mind, if your open position has a loss of 50% (that is, the price has fallen by half), then in order to restore the status quo, a price increase of 100% is required (that is, again, twice).

Therefore, the average loss per transaction should be significantly lower than the average profit. Therefore, if you bought a share at 200 dollars and set a "stop-loss" at 180, then the level where you are hoping to take profits should be at least 230, and preferably at least 240.

The most ingenious trader fails to make one profit - even the best traders, as a rule, have no more than 2/3 of successful transactions. A typical report on the work of a bad trader includes a large number of "small victories" and several huge losses that tremendously cover all winnings taken together. And these losses almost always occur precisely in those cases when the trader stubbornly continues to hold an open position, refusing to admit his mistake.

On the contrary, good traders, according to the results of their work, have a certain number of "small victories" and almost as many "small defeats" - but in addition to them, there are also very few "big victories" that bring the main profit. Do not be afraid of losses – learn how to work with them! Do not be a player - be a trader!

2. The trend is your friend

Do not trade against the trend! The idea of "catching" a global market turn and buying at the very minimum, of course, is very tempting - and more than one million traders have already managed to try it and burned out on such heroism.

3. Buy on rumors, sell on the news releases

Do not succumb to the magic of good news - they are often already expected by more experienced traders, including professional participants in the securities market. Therefore, such news is "played out" by the market in advance - the price rises for several days before the news. And when the latter really comes out, the price makes a small and short (in a minute or two) striker up - and begins to fall by throwing in amazement the newcomers who cannot understand why the market is falling on good news.

4. The market is always right

If the market goes down, then you can call the stupidity of its participants as much as you like - just do not try to expand this market. Your assessment of the situation may turn out to be incomplete - you might have missed something or even extremely dangerous pitfalls might have been hidden in the good news. Therefore, do not fight the market - it will cost you more.

5. Buy expensive, sell cheap

The message looks strange, but its meaning is simple. If the market broke through a strong and stubbornly defiant resistance level, then most likely it will grow for a long time. Therefore, in such cases, one should not be afraid that "it is already extremely expensive" - buy, and soon it will be even more expensive. The same goes for sales: a breakout of the level down gives a signal to sell. Do not hope for a quick turnaround out of considerations of "well, there's nowhere to get cheaper," there is always where to get cheaper.

6. Do not rush to buy when the collapse

Almost no one has yet succeeded in catching the falling knife - no analysis will show you the exact purpose of the sharp drop in price. The usual scheme is as follows: the collapse stops suddenly and is replaced by a sharp rebound in the price upwards. Then comes a return to the area of the previous minimum - and if at this moment the price has not broken even lower, then you can think about buying.

7. Use sliding stop level

It is often impossible to determine the goal of rising stock prices at the time of a strong trend - it just grows for itself and grows. The same goes for a sharp take-off - it is not clear whether continuation will follow after the inevitable rollback. Therefore, it is useful to use a moving level of exit from trading: put a mental barrier, say, 10-20 percent lower than the current price, and rearrange it higher and higher as the price rises. Then, with a trend reversal, you will not lose too much in comparison with the ideal option (that is, with the sale to the maximum) - and at the same time, avoid a hasty exit from a profitable position that could leave you too early in the market, continuing its rapid growth.

8. Never average a losing position!

Even some solid trading allowances recommend in case of a loss-making position to buy more so that the average purchase price is lower and in case of a bounce to the top, you quickly turn a profit. However, in practice, the price much more often continues to fall - and you simply get a double loss.

9. Do not give in to universal euphoria

After a long recovery, the market begins to fall precisely when the last "doubters" agree with the inevitability of further growth. If everyone is just buying, it makes sense to think about an early exit from the market. If you have 10 familiar analysts and all 10 predict strong growth, then the maximum of the market is already nearby, and the decline will begin soon.

10. Be consistent in your strategies!

If you have a trading system, follow it unconditionally, and do not choose whether to believe the system or better wait. If you have set a stop loss level, exit the market when it is reached, and do not try to push it "a little further". In any case, the results of a strategy can only be discussed with its consistent application. Otherwise, the result of your work will be a consequence of the overlapping mass of randomness - and that means, in the best case, this result will be zero.⏺

Beginner's mistakes to avoid

Making money on the stock exchange is a quite long process that requires the permanent development of both the trader himself and his trading strategy. Moreover, each trader in the process of becoming (and at the professional stage too) goes through a certain series of mistakes. He either learns from them or repeats them - until he identifies these errors and learns how to avoid them. As a result, he not only makes a profit but also turns trading into a category of truly creative activities.

Below you will find out the most frequent beginner's mistakes, learn them to be fully armed.

Trading on market opening during the first minutes of trading.

During this time the market usually fluctuates wildly or flies off somewhere (up or down) in no time. Sometimes, seasoned market participants try to take advantage of their knowledge to anticipate the market direction from the first minutes. For a novice trader, such an opportunity is excluded – your emotions can let you down.

Making haste in taking profits

You have bought a stock, it went up, after several days you checked out the money you earned - and happily closed the position. As it becomes clear later, this movement was only the start of a significant uptrend, so if you did not make haste, you could earn 10 times more. Only in exceptional cases, you can leverage take-profit orders - when an obvious level of resistance is visible. Generally, it is advisable to exit the market at a moving level of stop-loss.

Adding to a losing position

On the contrary: you have bought a stock, and the price went down. You stubbornly claim "it will grow anyway, I just hastened to open a position" - and keep on buying more. The price keeps on falling even further, simply doubling your losses. Keep in mind: Only a profitable position can be added.

Closing positions starting with the best

When you possess multiple purchases, and the price starts lowering, firstly you try to take profits by instinct and only then close the losing position (or leave it until the stop-loss order is executed). This is the wrong tactic: if the whole market went down, then most probably, those who behaved worse before, would fall faster than the others - and because of them you have a loss; thereby you must close this position first. Stocks that have grown, and now are likely to fall reluctantly, and if the market reverses, will go up again - so do not rush to close a profitable position.

Thirst for revenge

A typical novice's trick: a losing position has just closed - he again throws himself in the market excited to avenge his insult. The outcome will turn out in a new loss – so it is better not to come back to the market after the "catching loss". Take some rest.

The Presence of Highly Preferred Positions

Approach your positions wisely: for example, don't have any special sympathies for those you purchased at the very bottom-typically those purchases are a real pride to any trader! It's clear you 're overwhelmed with self-admiration – but don't bring such a great position to zero or even unprofitable. Get real.

Trading according to the principle "bought forever"

You worked in a relatively short period of time, bought a stock, and it suddenly rose rapidly. Then you say to yourself, "yeah, I caught the beginning of a long-term uptrend" - and suspend this position "forever". This does not happen, after all: either you toggle to much longer assessment periods, or you adopt your standard rules with your usual short period. Regulations can cause you to join and leave the business many times, including the case of a very strong pattern.

Closing a profitable strategic position on the first day

On the contrary, if you are not involved in trading within the day, then having opened up a serious position, under any circumstances do not close it on the first day. And if the price has risen so much-be careful, it will be much higher tomorrow.

Closing a position on a signal to open the opposite position

Many beginners trade in the non-stop market system. That is, such systems are always "in position": for them, closing a long position means opening a short one. It is possible to use such systems, but it should be closed earlier: the close signal should be harder than the signal to open the opposite position.

Hesitation

If you are not sure of your previous assessment of the situation then you cannot trade. Having said to yourself "vague doubts torment me," you must close all your positions on the spot and re-analyze the situation.

TOP 10 Movies about trading. A must watch for beginners

The Internet offers a lot of film collections on the trading topic, but how to understand what helps to expand knowledge in trading and get additional motivation. We collected 10 of the best movies that will help you to get the idea of trading and reach your financial goal.

1. Wall Street (1987)

This is an example of the very first films about trading and represents the classic of stock market filmography. The film describes a story about a young, enthusiastic broker who wishes to be successful against all odds. To do so, he begins a business collaboration with his idol, the stock exchange shark-Gordon Gecko, after which he is engaged in serious fraud.

2. Wall Street: Money Never Sleeps (2010)

After 23 years, the sequel "Wall Street: Money Does Not Sleep" is released. This film would also be useful for those who want to know more about stock market investing, but still, the sequel is drastically inferior to Wall Street's first segment.

3. The Big Short (2015)

The film helps to realize the causes of the 2008 mortgage crisis. The plot tells about several analysts who were able to foresee the recession and played for a fall while making a fortune.

4. Rogue Trader (1999)

The crime drama " Rogue Trader is interesting that it was shot on real events, according to Nick Leeson's book. It is based on the story of a bank clerk, who inflicted huge losses on one of the biggest banks, which led to bankruptcy.

5. Boiler Room (2000)

This film is most likely related to stock exchange issues, but watch a must if you are keen on trading. The film tells a story about a young man running an underground casino. He joined a brokerage firm but, in the end, his thirst for big money and greed played a cruel joke with him.

6. The Pursuit of Happiness (2006)

The movie tells about the man who went through a hard way and worked a great deal to become a successful broker starting from a poor sales representative.

7. The Wolf of Wall Street (2013)

The next movie that made our top is "The Wolf of Wall Street". Mostly it discloses the topic of exchange fraud. The film is based on real events and distinctly demonstrates that you have to pay for everything in the end.

8. Too Big to Fail (2011)

The film tells about the events due to which the financial collapse happened and escalated into the 2008 crisis. The plot is extremely gripping because the actions unfold around the Minister of Finance, who is trying to influence the financial catastrophe.

9. The Wizard of Lies (2017)

Another film deserving your attention is «The Wizard of Lies» This is a biographical film describing the major financial fraud of the 21st century, during which businessman Bernard Madoff managed to make fortune at the expense of his multimillion-dollar firm, that deserved a name of a financial pyramid.

10. Margin Call (2011)

This film shows a 24-hour time period during which bank employees, the prototype of which is Lehman Brothers, are trying to figure a way out of the crisis and avert bankruptcy.

Movies about trading are a great way to find out something new and relieve stress after a tensed trading day.

Property Investment

Chapter One:
Why Invest in Property?

There are far more reasons to invest in property than merely to generate income. While it is a lucrative market, the money is very rarely the be-all-end-all of real estate investment. Cash flow is important that much is certain, but there are so many other benefits that are often overlooked, which can have a significant impact on the investment experience.

When you choose your assets and priorities carefully, you can enjoy a cash flow that is predictable, tax advantages, excellent returns, and will be able to diversify your portfolio, while also being able to leverage your real estate to accumulate wealth. In this chapter, we are going to discuss a number of the many benefits to property investment, and how they can give you an advantage in the long run.

Cash flow

It goes without saying that the goal of every real estate investor that owns a rental property is to attain a positive cash flow on their investment property. Understanding the importance of cash flow and how it is calculated is vital, and finding solutions to cutting down the time it takes to calculate your cash flow can be even more important.

Calculating your properties' cash flow is perhaps the best way to determine its quality and estimating how profitable it can be. Most investment properties can have either a positive or negative cash flow, particularly with rental properties. If your goal is to make money by investing in real estate, you'll know that you have succeeded once you have one or more investment properties with a positive cash flow.

With a positive cash flow, your property makes money for you, regardless of how little the profit is. As long as you are achieving a positive cash flow with your property, you are safe. But, if your goal is to maximize your profits (which it probably is), you will need to understand what exactly cash flow is, and the ways that it influences your investment property.

What is Cash Flow, and how important is it for your Investment Property?

To put it simply, cash flow is the amount of profit that your investment property is making after you have calculated every expense that is related to your investment. Thus, a property with a positive cash flow is one that is producing more money than the sum of its expenses in one cycle.

Cycles are generally annually or monthly, but you'll find that the majority of property investors prefer the annual measurement for different reasons. The ability to calculate your investment property's cash flow is essential for successful real estate planning. This calculation helps estimate the possible expenses you may face and how they will affect you, as well as the influence they will have on the profitability of your real estate.

You'll be able to use these estimates to plan ahead and avoid situations in which your property will cause you to lose money suddenly. This is only possible because cash flow considers all of the expenses that can and will arise, even if you are unsure whether they will arise at all. This is where the difficulty occurs, as even though calculating cash flow may seem like a simple task, determining all of the possible expenses for your properties can be a hassle.

Later in this book, we are going to discuss how to calculate cash flow and cover a few of the possible expenses you may face when investing in property, especially as a novice.

Appreciation

Unfortunately, too many property investors do not know what to do with the potential price appreciation of their properties, so they simply do not take it into consideration. All too often, we tend only to focus on the cash flow from rental income, since it is arguably the easiest aspect to monitor. This makes it the only criterion that investors use to make decisions, and while it is the simpler method, it can also cost you hundreds of thousands of dollars.

Your rental property goal should not only be to achieve the highest cash flow. Instead, your goal should be the best risk-adjusted total return on your investment, assuming that the rental income covers your expenses. Merely assessing your cash flow to determine success and failure can be deceiving. You're able to more accurately determine what you need to do to achieve your financial goals when you analyze all of your profit centers, including cash flow, price appreciation, and tax savings.

Investment professionals have determined that real estate cycles will often repeat themselves every 10-20 years within a particular area or city. If you plan to maintain your properties for at least ten years and are familiar with the long-term historical appreciation rates, then you can expect a similar appreciation in the price of your property.

Diversifying your portfolio

Diversifying investment assets is vital to minimizing risk for every investor. By diversifying your property investment portfolio, you are essentially distributing your assets to reduce your overall risk of profit loss. To put it simply, if one property performs poorly during a cycle, but another performs better, your overall losses will be reduced.

How can you diversify your portfolio?

There are two main ways in which investors are able to diversify their property portfolio: by investing in different geographical locations, or by acquiring different property types. The latter is far more popular, as investing in another geographic location can be costly, and can make it challenging to prioritize.

Many amateur investors only consider apartments and houses when thinking about different types of properties. While building a diverse portfolio consisting of these assets can be effective, it is important to consider some of your other options as well. These options can include investing in townhouses and villas, in commercial property (directly or through a managed fund), or in residential development syndicates.

As with most things in the property investment industry, each of these properties come with their own pros and cons, so it's important to grasp each benefit and drawback, and how they work with your overall investment strategy. To put it into perspective, if you manage three homes in your portfolio, and they have high holding costs, it may be wise to buy an apartment or villa, since they generate higher cash flows thanks to their high rental incomes.

You could also diversify your portfolio by purchasing properties in different markets. You can do this by building a mixed portfolio consisting of properties in different capital city markets, whether in your home territory or not.

Most novice property investors will purchase their first few properties in their own capital city or region, generally in their own suburb, since they are familiar with the location. However, it is wise to begin looking at other markets after you have bought 3 - 4 properties in the same market, so that you may continue diversifying your portfolio.

This is extremely important because capital city property markets usually don't have aligned cycles. It means that property values in one market may be flourishing, while values in another market may plummet. This lets you distribute your risk by exposing yourself to several markets, offsetting any downfalls with increases.

Tax breaks and deductions

Property investment offers some excellent tax advantages that renting does not, but you'll need to understand how you can capitalize on these benefits. One of the greatest tax benefits for investors comes in the form of deductions, which are write-offs that include the costs associated with property tax, mortgage interest, operating expenses, and more.

What deductions can you make?

You are at liberty to deduct the necessary and regular expenses for managing and maintaining your property, as the property owner. These are considered *business finances* that will generally include property taxes, mortgage interest, maintenance, etc. As an investor, you're able to write off repairs, since they do not add value to a property, and serve only to keep them in good condition.

You can also deduct mortgage interest on your primary residences, and sometimes your secondary residence as well. Ensure that you carefully itemize your deductions. If you are thinking of starting a business, you should know that deductions can also come in the form of non-real estate activities, like using a home office. In most cases, you'll be able to deduct a portion of your home working expenses, like your phone bill and internet.

Investing in property can be beneficial in both the short and long term but determining what a meaningful goal is to you is what's most important. You also need to continually remind yourself that hardly anyone becomes an overnight millionaire through property investment. Doing so will help keep you motivated and inspired and will propel you towards reaching your goals.

Chapter Two:
A Diverse Market

As we've mentioned before, there is a lot more to property investment than simply owning a house or apartment and leasing it out. There are many other kinds of properties available to prospective investors, and there are several different ways in which one can invest in a property and generate income from it. Since this is a complete beginner's guide, we're going to cover the simpler investments you can make when entering the real estate field.

The different real estate investments

Residential

Residential properties are structures such as apartment buildings, houses, vacation houses, and townhouses, where an individual or group pays you to live in. The length of the stay, as well as the rent amount due each month, is determined by the rental or lease agreement. Most residential leases in the United States work off of a twelve-month basis.

Residential properties are perhaps the safest investments that new investors can make, which also makes them the most popular. They are generally less expensive to acquire than most of the other property types that we will discuss, depending on the area they are located in and the condition that they are in when you purchase them.

Residential properties usually also require less hands-on maintenance, since the tenants that stay there will generally keep it in good condition. However, you cannot rely on tenants to do this all the time, and some tenants may even let the property deteriorate over the course of their stay. It will then be up to you to restore the property once their lease has ended, which can cost you precious time and money.

However, you'll find that most tenants avoid letting this happen, so it's quite a rare scenario.

Commercial

Commercial properties are also fairly popular real estate investment options and consist mainly of skyscrapers and office buildings. If you were to acquire or construct a small building with individual offices within, you could lease each individual office to small business owners and companies who would pay rent to use the property. It is quite common for commercial properties to use multi-year leases since they can provide a stable cash flow, and sometimes even protect the owner from the decline of rental rates.

However, prospective investors should always keep in mind that markets will fluctuate, and rental rates may significantly increase over a short period. But you might be unable to raise your rental rates if your commercial property is bound by older agreements. Commercial buildings generally require a greater level of involved maintenance, as they are quite a bit larger than residential properties.

Retail

Retail properties include things like strip malls, shopping malls, and other smaller retail storefronts. Similarly to residential properties, retail locations do not require much hands-on maintenance from the owner, as tenants generally like to keep their stores as clean and orderly as possible.

In some cases, you, as the owner will receive a percentage of the income generated by the tenant store's sales, in addition to the base rent, which will provide an incentive for the tenant to keep the property as pristine as possible. Retail property investment, especially in smaller storefronts, can be unpredictable, as the tenant relies solely on the sales they make to pay their rent to you. If a store runs out of stock or loses customers, they will not be able to pay their rent, and they will have to move out.

This is why it's recommended that beginner investors avoid jumping into a retail investment, and instead opt for residential or commercial investments, where a stable income is almost guaranteed.

Industrial

Perhaps the most lucrative property investment, industrial real estate, includes storage units, warehouses, car washes, and any other special-purpose property that generates sales from customers that make use of the facility. For example, if you were to acquire a car wash, you could install some coin-operated vacuum cleaners, which would increase the return on your investment.

Mixed-Use

As the name suggests, mixed-use properties are lots that combine any of the categories mentioned above into one project. These types of properties are popular amongst investors that have access to significant access and cash, as they have a level of diversification that is built-in, which, as we have mentioned in the previous chapter, is important to control risk.

The different ways to invest in property

There are a couple of other ways to successfully invest in property other than becoming a landlord, like house flipping or real estate investment groups. Let's discuss some of them:

Becoming a Landlord

By far the most popular way to invest in real estate, becoming a landlord ensures that you have total control over your property, and how it generates income for you. However, you will need a substantial sum of capital to be able to finance some of the initial costs for maintenance, and also to cover any vacant months (or months where your property is not generating income). Rental properties can provide a regular income to landlords, while also using leverage to maximize their available capital.

What's more, many of the expenses that are associated with rental properties are tax-deductible, and most gains can be offset with losses with other investments. In the ideal situation, rental properties can appreciate in value over the duration of their mortgages, which leave landlords with an asset more valuable than when they started.

The drawback comes in when we consider maintenance. Unless you employ a company to manage your properties for you, rentals will often cause headache after headache. In the worst scenarios, unruly tenants could cause damage to your property. Additionally, in certain rental market environments, you as a landlord will need to charge less rent or bear vacancies so that you can cover expenses until the situation improves.

On a more positive note, as soon as the mortgage is paid off in full, most of the rent becomes profit entirely.

House Flipping

House flipping is more for folks who have significant experience in real estate marketing and evaluation, as well as expertise in renovation. To flip houses, you will need some capital, and will also need to be able to oversee or perform repairs as they are needed.

There is a shorter period during which effort and capital are tied up in a property when flipping houses, though, depending on the conditions of the market, you can receive significant returns, even in shorter time frames. However, trading real estate requires a more in-depth knowledge of the market, and there is a certain degree of pure luck involved, making it a field better-suited to more experienced property investors.

Real Estate Investment Groups

REIGs are perfect for those that wish to own rental properties without needing to deal with running them. They require a 'capital cushion' and sufficient funding and are a far less involved approach to property investment that can still provide appreciation and income.

There is, unfortunately, a risk of vacancy when working with real estate investment groups, whether it is specific to the owner or distributed throughout the group. In theory, such groups are a safe way to invest in property, but in practice, they are susceptible to similar fees that the mutual fund industry faces.

Furthermore, REIGs are occasionally private investments that dishonest management teams use to swindle money from their investors. Therefore, you will need to be meticulous when choosing a real estate investment group to avoid the risk of being scammed as much as possible.

REIGs are similar to mutual funds that invest in rental real estate. Standard real estate investment groups lease a property in the name of the investor, and each unit pools a part of the rent as a kind of safeguard against any occasional vacancies that may occur. This allows you to receive a bit of income, even if your property is vacant. There should be enough to cover costs, provided that the vacancy rates for the pooled units do not get too high.

It's clear to see that the property investment industry is exceptionally diverse, and there are plenty of options available out there to prospective investors. The different investment and property types that we have mentioned above one just a few of many, and could write a separate book on each of them. Choosing the right one to start with can make or break your property investment career, so it's recommended that you consider one that we mentioned above.

Chapter Three:
Creating a Business Plan

All successful businesses start with a plan, and pretty much anyone who achieves great success started out with one that is solid and comprehensive. Even if you plan something simple, it is still a statement of what you intend to do with your business, and how you plan on making it profitable. The vast majority of novice property investors looking to enter the industry, start without even a basic plan, which ultimately leads to failure.

It often feels as though we're sitting around and wasting our time creating a plan when we could be out there looking at properties and start making money. But it's important to realize that almost everyone who does not begin with a plan ends up disappointed and dissatisfied, regardless of the amount of time and effort they put in.

What is a property investment business plan, and what does it look like?

There's no need to create hundreds of pages of fancy charts and projections when developing your property investment business plan. On the contrary, the best business plan would be one so simple that it could fit on a single page so that you're able to memorize it and use it to motivate each decision you make.

In order to achieve such simplicity, you will have to think long and hard about your priorities. Below is an example of what your business plan could look like:

Current Budget	$100 000
Goal Profits	$50 000
Current Debt	$75 000
Current properties owned	1
Current Property Types	Residential, Commercial
Goal Properties	3

Of course, your plan does not have to be identical to this, and you should take the time to personalize it to your goals, making it as brief or extensive as you'd like. The key is creating a plan that is easy for you to understand, interpret, and follow. Your goals should also be realistic, as setting unattainable goals will inevitably leave you feeling dejected and without motivation.

Where are you currently?

It's impossible to plan ahead if you don't know where you're starting from. Determining your point of origin is the easiest part of creating a business plan because it consists of information that you either already know, or that is easy for you to learn. You need to consider things like the amount of money that you have available to invest, how much of your savings can be put towards property investment in the future, and the time you're able to invest each week or month.

The thing that makes this part of your business plan difficult is the fact that you need to be honest to yourself about what you can commit, and knowing yourself well enough to see what your strengths are. Knowing how much money you have to invest should not be a problem, but you may want to consult with a mortgage broker to see your borrowing options.

This will help you figure out your total investment figure. Brokers are also able to inform you about the options that are available to you regarding releasing equity from your own home if that is something you wish to do. You should also consider keeping an emergency fund in cash and deduct that amount from your total investment budget.

Having around half a year's expenses in the bank at all times will act as a safeguard if your plan ever fails. Pouring every cent to your name into your investments very rarely ends well - you still want to be able to pay your bills.

Where do you want to go?

Now that you have an idea of your starting point, it's time to look at where you want to be in the future, or what are your **goals?** Of course, you want to be secure or rich, or you want to build a future. Who doesn't? But you'll need to know what that means and what it looks like to you in terms of cash. You also need to figure out when you want to achieve these goals.

There is a lot of thought involved in figuring these things out the proper way. Being general is not useful - you need to take an honest look at your ideal lifestyle and come up with a figure that is truly meaningful to you, regardless of how big or small it is. The same also goes for the time you want to take to reach your goals, as it can drastically influence even your most basic investment decisions.

Here's an example to help put things into perspective:

Property A provides a return of 12% on your investment, but it is highly unlikely that it will ever increase in value.

On the other hand, *Property B* provides an 8% return on your investment, but could possibly double in value during the next decade.

If your goal is to generate a specific income each month within four years, then *Property A* will probably be your best choice. It is unlikely for any major growth to occur during that time, so you will need to prioritize money in your bank now.

Otherwise, if your goal spans more than a decade, you would likely find *Property B* to be more beneficial. Investing in this property is a small risk in terms of growth on capital, but there is a lot of time for it to happen, and when it eventually does happen, your returns will make the higher rental income from *Property A* look like pocket change.

By this point in the planning process, you may realize that the gap between where you are and where you want to be, seems almost too vast. It probably seems impossible to reach your goals with the resources you currently have at your disposal. This is why it is now time to start thinking of a strategy you will use to pursue and achieve your goal.

Investment strategies and how you can use them

When you are creating a property investment business plan, you have to take into consideration which kind of investment strategy will suit your goals the best. We are going to take a look at a few strategies that are **proven** to be effective, as well as some of their pros and cons.

Professional Single Lets

This is by far the most commonly used investment strategy and succeeds the most often as well. Buying a property and renting it out to a tenant can generate income in one of two ways - the growth in the property's capital value over time, and the monthly rental income after the deduction of expenses.

Professional single lets are the 'traditional' buy-to-let method, which involves renting out a property to a working family or individual as a single unit. It has been around for ages and is the simplest form of property investment there is. You just need to get your calculations correct the first time, buy in a good area or region, rent the property to a tenant, and ensure that they are gladly paying their rent on time.

This is a gross simplification, but this is all that is at the core of professional single let renting. While we are going to cover a few more advanced property investment strategies, this is the one that most property investors use and is one of the most effective as well, which lends to its popularity.

Pros:

- Simplest investment strategy

- Very little management time required

- Easy to acquire mortgages for

- Predictable returns

Cons:

- Lower returns than other strategies

Holiday Lets

As you may have guessed, holiday lets are properties that are rented out over short periods to holidaymakers. They are also sometimes called 'serviced accommodations,' which are essentially the same things, but with a target demographic of business travelers in urban areas. There is quite a bit of intersection between these terms, and their basic structures are the same - the difference lies in the type of customer that is targeted.

If you're able to achieve a high occupancy level with this strategy, the profits can be incredible. A cottage near the sea, for example, can be quite easy to fill up during the warmer months of the year, but you can make even more money if you're able to keep it occupied throughout the rest of the year, even if you have to lower your rates somewhat.

The only real downside to this strategy is that it requires pretty much round-the-clock work, with frequent occupancy changes and marketing to consider. It can also be quite challenging to find a mortgage that will permit lets for such short terms, so the return on your investment might be even lower with a high rental income due to reduced leverage.

Pros:

- No secure tenure = no need for evictions

- High occupancy yields high returns

- Better tax deductions

Cons:

- Requires year-round work

HMOs

In essence, HMOs are shared homes that are rented per room to unrelated tenants. There are a number of separate definitions for what exactly constitutes an HMO, but we'll stick with the basic definition for the purpose of this guide.

On average, renting out a property by the room can generate more revenue than if you were to rent it out as a whole. However, they also come with higher costs, since HMOs are usually furnished, and include bills - and there is often more wear and tear to these properties. Managing an HMO can definitely be more time consuming, meaning your letting agent fees could be higher, or you as a landlord may need to be more involved.

Even after you have taken these extra costs into consideration, HMOs can offer a higher yield, which has caused them to surge in popularity over the last few years. However, this means that councils have also taken more action to regulate them by increasing the types of HMOs that need to be licensed, making existing regulations more thorough, and denying access to the development of new HMOs in certain areas.

Pros:

- Diverse stream of income

- Greater yield than single lets

Cons:

- More regulations

- Requires more thorough management

There are many more property investment strategies out there that come with their own benefits and drawbacks - those mentioned above are merely the most popular and have the highest rates of success, especially for investors just entering the market. While you are under no obligation to make use of one of these strategies are highly recommend that you do, as they are guaranteed to be profitable.

Chapter Four:
Investing in Your First Property

Now that you are familiar with the very basics of property investment, it's time to learn how to invest in your first property. Making your first real estate investment is both an exciting and stressful time. It can be incredibly taxing to move from one house show to the next in between your daily tasks, but signing your name on the sales contract is one of the most satisfying feelings ever, and makes it all worth it.

In this chapter, we're going to look at how you can achieve your investment dreams through careful planning and consideration. The process is fairly simple, but it requires plenty of effort and critical thinking.

Get out of debt

Easier said than done, right? This first step is the most important in this process since your credit score is the first thing that is evaluated when applying for a home loan. If you are still deep in debt, it might be quite challenging for you to receive approval for your bond.

If you still find yourself struggling to repay your credit card accounts, student loans, or medical bills, then investing in real estate might not be the wise thing to do at this stage in your life. Consider getting advice from a debt counselor on how you can pay off your debt in the shortest amount of time, then consider property investment.

If you currently earn enough money to pay off all of your outstanding debts, and the monthly mortgage costs and those related as well, then you are free to start considering acquiring your first investment property.

Understand the difference between your first home and an investment property

This may be obvious to some, but it's worth mentioning anyway. After all, this is a guide for total beginners. There is a very clear difference between making your first property investment and buying your primary residence. The former will, hopefully, provide you with a constant flow of income through rental payment and a profit once you sell it, while the latter is the place in which you'll live permanently.

Understanding this difference *before* you begin searching for a property is vital because there are several various factors that you'll have to take into consideration before you make your purchase. These factors will include things like proximity to general services, work, and family, or the number of rooms you need in a property.

All of these things will have some impact on your decision-making process when buying your primary residence but will probably not influence your decision when acquiring an investment property. Investment properties will often be the cheaper of these two options since they won't have to meet all the requirements for an ideal home.

You will also need to pay the Capital Gains Tax when selling an investment property, which you will not have to pay if and when you decide to sell your primary residence. You can also make the distinction based on your emotions - buying your primary residence is more of an emotional decision than buying an investment property, as you'll be considering the space that your loved ones will be living in.

Realize that managing a property requires a lot of effort

As we have discussed a few times before, being a landlord can and will be a very time-consuming task, especially if you work a full-time job as well. If you thought that finding a property was difficult, wait until you have to start managing one.

Tenants can be quite demanding sometimes, especially if your property has a faulty feature or fixture - they'll probably want it fixed immediately. This is fair since you would probably want your landlord to fix any problems your rented property might have as well. You will encounter at least one tenant during your property investment career that will be late on their rent payments, and sometimes not pay rent at all.

This can be incredibly frustrating, especially if you only own one investment property that is the sole source of your cash flow. But it's important to be patient, and hiring a rental agent that acts as the middleman between you and your tenant/s can help ease some of the stress. Living on-site can be beneficial as well, as you'll be more inclined to keep your property pristine, and it could help reduce travel costs as well.

Pay attention to location

You've probably heard the phrase 'location, location, location' at least once in your life, but do you know what it actually means? Most people don't, because there are several factors that determine whether or not a location can be considered 'good', most of which are very subjective.

The safest bet is to choose a location that is close to amenities like stores and public transports. Places near universities are ideal as well, because most students will rent your property for the duration of their time studying at the university, and their parents will generally provide some personal guarantees on the rent.

Finding a good location will ensure that you receive some good returns on your investment, and can improve the resale value of your property as well. Gentrified areas, or areas that have been developed to be comfortable to the middle class are also becoming popular amongst property investors since properties within them cost less to acquire and appreciate in value faster. Remember to only explore options in locations that you can comfortably afford, or you risk putting yourself in a dangerous situation, however tempting it may be.

Examine the economic cycle at present

The economic cycle can be thought of in three stages, and first-time property investors should pay careful attention to these stages, and the cycle as a whole. The first stage in the economic cycle is the **Recession Stage,** which is the best and scariest time to acquire property. Unemployment and inflation are high in this stage, and the demand for rental properties tends to decline.

The next stage is the **Recovery Stage,** in which rental rates begin to increase once more, and the number of vacancies starts to decrease. Finally, we reach the third and final stage, called the **Peak Stage.** In this stage, you'll notice an increase in interest rates, an increase in the number of new projects, and a rise in inflation. Some markets can experience a leveling of prices and increased rates of vacancy.

Source service providers that are trustworthy and professional

As a property investor, one of your responsibilities will be to accumulate a list of professional service providers that you can trust. These should include accountants, lawyers, and tradesmen like plumbers and electricians. The easiest way to do this is to talk to your friends.

They are likely to know at least one person who can help you and will be able to provide you with their contact details if you just ask. You could also turn to the internet, which has a wealth of property professionals looking for clients. Just make sure that you read any business reviews they may have, and see what other people are saying and if they can be trusted.

Or, if this all sounds a little too challenging or time-consuming, you could hire a property manager, though they might be quite costly for a prospective property investor just entering the field.

Acquire financing for your property

If you are going to pay for your investment property in cash, then you don't need to follow this step. Otherwise, you will need to find a way to get money for your purchase. Financing a primary residence and financing an investment property are two very different processes. You will need excellent qualifications since lenders generally consider mortgages for investment properties riskier than loans on properties occupied by the owner.

You have a few options for financing your investment property, and you should consider having a preapproval for a loan regardless of which you choose. Otherwise, you should have financing secured *before* you begin browsing properties.

Conventional financing - this blanket term refers to a mortgage that is obtained from a bank and is backed up by your personal qualifications. There are a number of factors that determine the requirements for conventional financing, like your credit score, the property type, and your employment status. Conventional loans are generally the most effective way to go if you are able to qualify for one.

Asset-based loans - this is the main alternative to conventional loans, and, as the name suggests, the qualifications for this loan depend on the asset in question (the investment property in this case) rather than the qualifications of the borrower. In other words, asset-based lenders will check your credit score to see if you are eligible, but they will not look at your income, debts, or employment status.

The main condition is that your property will need to generate enough cash flow to cover the payments for the mortgage, with a realistic cushion as well. The lender will make use of what is known as the DSCR, or the Debt Service Coverage Ratio.

Choose a mortgage type and develop a comprehensive lease

There are several options available to you when deciding on a type of mortgage, like paying the loan back over either 15 or 30 years or having a fixed or adjustable rate. In the case of most mortgages, you will be required to provide a deposit of at least 5% towards the property.

The goal is to pay the least amount possible upfront since your payments will be lower if your deposit is a large sum. You should also keep in mind that your mortgage costs might not fully be covered by your rental price.

After you have acquired your first investment property, you will begin the next cycle of property investment, which mostly consists of finding a tenant that is suitable for your property. Be sure to draft a legal lease agreement with your lawyer when doing so.

This lease should include things like a summary of the fees such as water and electricity, policies regarding pets, subletting, and misconduct, etc., penalties for breaching the lease, as well as methods and due dates for payments.

Below is a checklist that you can use to determine whether or not you meet the requirement that you'll need to invest in your first property.

Property Checklist

☐ Debt-free

☐ Know the difference between a primary residence
and an investment property

☐ Prepared for the effort required of a landlord

☐ Found an ideal location

☐ Considered and understand the current economic
cycle

☐ Sourced professional, trustworthy service providers
(lawyers, accountants, electricians, etc.)

☐ Sourced secure financing OR have sufficient finances
already

☐ Settled on a mortgage type

☐ Developed a comprehensive lease

☐ Acquired my first investment property!

Once you've checked every box on this list, you'll be ready to acquire your first property and then move onto the next chapter, in which we'll discuss how you can generate as much profit as possible.

Chapter Five:

Maximizing Your Profits

If there's one thing that we know for certain, it's that you are interested in the property investment industry for one thing: PROFIT. We all want to be rich, and while real estate won't make us millionaires overnight, it can get us a lot of money in a relatively short amount of time. Your investment should be generating at least a 6%-8% return.

The three main factors that will have a positive impact on the profits that you earn are **occupancy, maintenance,** and **on-time payments.** This includes every rental property you have in your portfolio, regardless of whether you manage them yourself, or via a management company. If you are using a managing company, and they aren't helping you make *% returns, then you need to review the way they are managing your properties.

Key Question: Why aren't you achieving maximum profits?

There are a few things that are likely preventing you from achieving that 6-8% return margin. We are going to discuss them below, and how you can remedy them and maximize your profits.

Inadequate tenant screening, or none at all

Tenant screening should be at the top of your list of priorities as a rental property owner. Your investment can only ever be profitable if you are leasing your properties to tenants that pay their rent on time and do not cause damage to your real estate. You could even consider collecting a security deposit to cover the property damage costs, but the overhead and time required to perform property repairs will chew through your income.

There are a couple of options available to monitor the bill-paying habits of your future tenants. You can view their credit reports, assess their tendency to follow the rules by browsing their criminal background and contacting previous landlords, and review their bank statements to see how much money they earn.

You would be shocked at just how many landlords don't take advantage of these basic practices for screening tenants. There are quality background checks and tenant credit checks for as little as $15, and this small investment is well worth it to prevent any potential loss of rent from a tenant who does not may and any dangerous activity that you may have to deal with.

Tenants that are responsible, and that have a verifiable bill-paying and rule-complying history will ensure that you have a positive tenant-landlord relationship, which subsequently maximizes the amount of cash you receive.

Online rent payments mean fewer late payments

Stop wasting time with those pesky deposit checks and have your tenants pay online, which will also avoid sitting through excuses like 'it was lost in the mail'. Smart investors value their time just as much as they do their other assets. There exist various software solutions that are designed to enable renters to streamline their rental management. One of the best and newest of these technologies is the ability to make rental payments online.

Not only do online rent payments make the rent collection process exquisitely simple, but they also make life easier for your tenants as well. It may sound silly, but the rent check that your tenants pay is normally the largest bill they pay each month, and writing that check out can be stressful, even emotional sometimes. Online payments can lower this stress significantly, especially when using automatic payment systems.

You should also ensure that your automatic bill payments are set up as well, so you don't miss any bills that you might have otherwise. You can also sometimes negotiate a discount with online services for paying your bills, which will reduce your overall operating costs and increase your profits even more.

Relying on tenants to maintain your properties

This problem is no more your fault than it is your tenants. People are forgetful, particularly in the rushed working world of today. Your tenants might not be familiar with what they need to do to keep a home free of damage via routine maintenance, especially if they are young adults.

You have no control over how your tenants will use features or fixtures in your property, especially regarding appliances like refrigerators and thermostats. Even if you are totally confident that all your bases are covered by requiring tenants to perform basic maintenance, they will probably still forget.

That's why it is up to you to invest some money and time into routine service and maintenance checkups on the main appliances in your properties. This will extend the life of such appliances, like ovens, air conditioning, washers, dryers, and so on. The same can be said for seasonal maintenance.

It's one thing to state in your lease that tenants should trim the trees and clean the driveway, but you will face a much more costly bill if they fail to do so than if you were to send over a seasonal landscaper annually, who would be able to perform these maintenance tasks. You need to make your maintenance expectations crystal-clear to your tenants, and they need to know exactly what they are expected to take care of.

You should also remind them every now and then about when and how they need to do these tasks. Set reminders on your phone's calendar for every season to do things like change an air filter or clean the gutters. Allow your tenants to easily and conveniently submit requests for maintenance if you're looking to keep damage to your property at a minimum. Software that offers a tenant portal online is one easy solution, as it will let your renters submit maintenance requests straight from their smartphones. The easier it is for tenants to report maintenance issues, the more likely they are to take the time to report them.

Increase the rent

This may seem obvious but increasing the rent that tenants will pay to stay on your investment properties will increase the profits that you make. Increases in rent keep your property within the market value price, allow you to reach rates that are profitable, and help you stay on top of your expenses.

The key to increasing your rent successfully is by getting as little backlash from your tenants as you can. The increase should meet the demands of the market, but it should not be so extreme that your tenants are not able to afford it and move out, which would result in a vacancy and a decrease in profits. Building regular increases in rent into your lease agreement is the easiest way to present approachable increases.

By doing this, you are allowing your tenants to prepare for these living expenses raises so that they can budget accordingly.

Permit pets

The vast majority of us have pets, and we all know how difficult it is to find housing that is pet-friendly. As an investor, you are given the opportunity to capitalize on this demand for housing that accommodates pets, by allowing tenants to have pets on your property, with rules that are clearly outlined, and a higher rent amount.

You could possibly charge a monthly rent for pets on the property if your tenant owns any, which is an easy way to get additional income from that property. If the pet ever causes damage to your property, which is very unlikely, then you will still be able to deduct the necessary amount from the tenant's security deposit.

However, you should know that **emotional support animals and service animals are not considered pets, and you are not allowed to charge additional fees for these types of animals.**

Offer more services

If you own a triplex, fourplex, or multi-family property, you might be able to increase your profits via coin-operated laundry machines. Providing an on-site laundry facility can make your property more appealing, especially if the property does not provide an in-unit washer or dryer.

You can lease these machines from major appliance companies, or you could buy the machines yourself and keep all of the profits, but you'd need to maintain them yourself as well. Also, keep in mind any other laundry facilities in the neighborhood, as well as water costs, to ensure that having an on-site laundry facility will benefit both you and your tenants.

Keep up-to-date with maintenance

One of the best and most effective ways to increase the lifespan and profitability of your properties is to keep them routinely maintained. As an investor, it is your responsibility to be very diligent when it comes to maintenance since you are not always going to be on your property, ensuring that routine tasks are being done.

Landlords also need to inform their tenants about how important it is that they maintain the property to some extent. This should all be outlined in your lease agreement, even if doing so may seem obvious. Being diligent with routine seasonal maintenance will save you a lot of money, and will help you avoid the cost of contractors who will need to fix a feature or appliance that would have lasted longer had you otherwise maintained them properly.

Work with a team that you trust

There will be times when you have to hire a professional to fix something, regardless of how well you and your tenants worked to maintain your property. Knowing the right vendors and contractors and being able to get a hold of them quickly, will help keep your costs as low as possible when an issue with maintenance arises.

Having good relationships with electricians, plumbers, painters, and various other home maintenance professionals and vendors will give you quick and easy access to the right services when they are needed. If your tenant contacts you with an emergency regarding maintenance, you will be able to call the appropriate maintenance professional and can pay them a favorable price.

The last thing you want to do is call around in an effort to find someone who is available when you need them to handle your emergency. It is at this point that maintenance can become incredibly expensive.

By now, you may have noticed that the best way to maximize your profits is not to increase the amount of money you are receiving each month, but rather to decrease your costs for the upkeep of your properties. Keep your expenses low and reserve fund topped-up by taking the time to screen tenants and eliminating potential damage to your property.

Chapter Six:

Maintaining Your Property

Taking care of your investment properties is just as important as acquiring them, if not more. Your real estate needs meticulous care and special attention to become successful and stay that way, as with most things in life. We're going to take a look at some of the things you can do to ensure that your properties are always in the best condition they can be, and how you can maintain a consistent occupancy.

Inspecting the interior and exterior of your properties

A well-kept property that is free of any kind of damage will help raise your profits and keep good tenants. As we discussed in the previous chapter, some maintenance tasks are inevitable, and your properties will become damaged in some way throughout the course of your investment career. Being able to closely inspect your properties for any damages, no matter how minor they may be, is a vital skill that can spell the difference between a good landlord, and an excellent one.

Be sure to **check all of the windows** and see if they are sealed correctly, with no gaps in any of the panes or fillings. If there are gaps, fill them. Doing so will save you plenty of money in the future that would otherwise have to be spent on heat loss and damage caused by moisture.

Check the roof for any tiles or shingles that may be missing, and mold or moss, and for any flashing that has been damaged. While these may seem like minor things that don't require immediate attention, they can cause some serious damage that will cost you a small fortune to repair. You should also check if there are any tree limbs that have grown onto your roof. If there are, cut them off, so that they don't scratch the roof, or fall off. They are also quite unattractive and can be a deterrent for tenants.

Look for any **broken tree limbs** or **trees with fungal growths.** These things can be dangerous to the tenant living on the property, so you'll want to deal with them immediately. Also, make sure that the lawn is healthy and that the grass is mowed regularly - this will let any potential tenants know that you are dedicated to keeping your property maintained.

Ensure that **the exterior walls are always painted** to prevent any sun or moisture damage to the property. If your house doesn't look good, nobody will want to live in it.

Regarding the interior of the property, you will want to ensure that there are **smoke detectors** in the kitchen and that they always have new, working batteries. Non-functional smoke detectors pose a serious threat to tenants, so keeping them up and running is essential.

The **water heater should be kept clean** at all times. Drain it and remove any dirt on a regular basis, especially if your property is located in an area with a lot of sediment in the water.

Inspect the heating and cooling system regularly, and make sure that there are no plants or fungi growing around its filters. They can restrict the flow of air and can damage the system beyond repair, which will cost you a lot of money to replace.

Keeping your tenants happy and satisfied

Keeping your tenants happy is just as important as keeping your property in pristine condition, with the latter having a major impact on the former. If your tenants are satisfied, they will be more inclined to keep your property maintained, which saves you the hassle and cost of having to repair damages yourself.

A simple checkup every once in a while to see how things are going, or asking if there's anything that they need will be more than enough. Showing your tenants that you care about their comfort and that you are willing to help them through any property-related stresses that their satisfaction is your priority will make all the difference in the world.

This also boosts your reputation with future tenants and will make you a magnet for prospective renters.

Make sure that you respond to their maintenance requests. One of the leading causes of tenants moving out is dissatisfaction, so keep them pleased as much as possible.

Follow the Landlord-Tenant law

The landlord-tenant law outlines the rights and obligations that each party has regarding a rental property. Both the tenant and the landlord will need to know the basics of renting a home, how to pay or collect security deposits, and much more.

Newer landlords will likely need help working out their tax deductions or figuring out how to go about evicting a tenant because of unpaid rent. On the other hand, tenants might need assistance with understanding their right to safety as a tenant, how their security deposits are returned, and whether they are able to sublet a property.

Following the landlord-tenant law will aid you in maintaining your investment property and correctly managing it. It provides a basic structure for both you and your tenant so that neither of you makes any mistakes, and you're able to keep your property in good condition. Under this law, the tenant is obligated to maintain the property that they are renting, which is a huge bonus for landlords, especially those who have a number of properties that require micromanaging.

Hire a property manager

This may be a bit of a costly task for beginner property investors, but if you are able to afford a property manager, you can gain access to a host of benefits. By now, you will have noticed that taking care of a property is a lot of work, and it can often feel overwhelming.

Property managers help relieve some of this stress by essentially maintaining your investment real estate for you. Hiring one is a big decision to make, as the services they provide come with a steep price tag attached, but you'll be saving yourself a lot of time if you do. Property managers can do everything from handling the rent to touching up the interior and exterior of your property.

Renovations and improvements

Prospective tenants are continually looking for new and developed properties available for rent. As a landlord, it is essential that you always consider ways that you can renovate and improve your investment properties. Doing so will increase their value and will attract tenants who may be interested in renting your property.

Some renovating ideas include fixing up the bathrooms by either replacing the old fixtures with new and improved versions or changing the appearance of the bathroom to something more modern. You could remove the carpeting in the house and switch it out for hardwood flooring, which is more attractive and hygienic since there will be no fibers for dirt to cling to.

You could also consider upgrading the kitchen with newer appliances, and add some more non-essential ones like a coffee machine. Kitchen and bathroom renovation can be either very cheap or extremely expensive, but both options will increase the value of your property.

Why is it important to maintain your investment property?

Keeping your property in top shape has a number of benefits. The first and most obvious is that it will help you avoid any additional costs. Ensuring that you fix a problem early will reduce the number of problems you'll have to deal with in the future significantly, which subsequently reduces the number of your expenses.

Keeping a strict maintenance routine will let both you and your tenant know that your real estate is always ready for service. Keeping your property maintained will also attract good tenants. If your property is poorly kept when you are trying to get a tenant to move in, you might start to attract unruly tenants who could damage your real estate. A good property can also yield more rental income as well.

Chapter Seven:
Managing Your Finances

We've discussed profits, expenses, and income in great detail so far, but now it's time to take things one step further and talk about how you should be managing your finances to become a successful property investor. Whether your investment goals are long-term or short-term, you should always look at your investment over the long term, using a ten-year view, especially if your strategy is to buy and maintain property.

Finance is just as important as choosing a property, as we've said time and time again, and it can often even be more important. The volume of property that you're able to acquire depends on how much financing you can borrow or generate - if you don't get your finances ordered, you may bottleneck your ability to expand and diversify your investment portfolio.

More often than not, you are going to need to borrow money from a bank in order to finance a property purchase. This amount of debt that you will require is also known as **the level of gearing.** The higher this level, the higher your risk of financial troubles, should you lose a tenant, or if interest rates were to increase. The main advantage that gearing provides is that the interest you pay is tax-deductible, making the investment more tax-efficient overall.

Some finance tips

The advice below can be applied anywhere in your property investment career, whether you are just starting out or whether you have been in the industry for a decade. Properly managing your finances will only ever be beneficial in both the short term and long term. Here are a few ways that you can manage your finances:

Consolidate your debts

We've already discussed this matter in *Chapter Four,* but ensuring that all of your debt is paid off before you invest in a property, whether it's your first or your tenth, will allow you to borrow more money from the bank. This subsequently lets you purchase more high-end properties, or put more cash towards renovating and improving your existing properties, which increases their value and causes them to appreciate quicker.

If you have multiple outstanding loans, make sure that you pay off the ones with the highest interest rates first, since they cost you the most in the long run. High-interest loans also impact your borrowing capacity the most, which is why getting them out of the way should be one of your priorities.

Cancel unused credit cards and reduce credit card limits

If truly honest, credit cards are poison. Yes, they're useful, and yes, they can get us out of a tight situation in a pinch, but they can also often lead to some crippling debt, especially if you get into the habit of overspending. Reducing the limit on your credit card or cards can make a massive difference to the amount of money you are able to borrow for your property. If you have some credit cards that you are not using, you should consider canceling them, since lenders will take your credit cards into account when calculating how much you are able to borrow, even if you aren't using them.

I recommend having a maximum of two credit cards. Try to have one for spending on improving your existing properties, while using the other to acquire more property. This will be a form of financial management without much planning.

Use different lenders

Convenience and loyalty are the main reasons that people tend to stick with the same lender each time they need to borrow money. However, this ultimately decreases the amount of money that you are allowed to borrow and increases your risks. When one lender funds your entire portfolio, they begin to assess your properties a whole instead of individually.

Using separate lenders lets you track down the best deal possible, keeping you in total control of your assets, and, most important, y increases your borrowing capabilities.

Plan!

There's a reason that I dedicated an entire chapter to creating a business plan (see: *Chapter Three)*. As the old saying goes, 'fail to plan, and you plan to fail.' This is especially true in the property investment industry since you are often working with large sums of money that need to be carefully spent.

As with any other successful business, investors need to develop detailed and comprehensive plans that outline the strategies that will allow them to grow their property portfolio. Not only that, but it will help them plan and manage the finances that will be needed to achieve their goals, and should provide an analysis of cash flow and how costs like debt are going to be taken care of.

Avoid cross-collateralization

Cross-collateralization is the term that is used when the collateral for one loan becomes the collateral for another, separate loan. If you were to borrow a home loan and use your house as security, or borrow a car loan and use your car as security, from the same bank, those assets could be used as *cross-collaterals* for both loans, and so on.

This can cause some tremendous issues when your properties start to appreciate in value, and you want to release some of the equity that has been generated. The lender has your assets all tied up, meaning that if you wanted to consult another lender that offers a better deal, your current lender might not partly discharge their mortgage so that you could refinance the property.

Additionally, if you wish to sell a portion of your property portfolio to help consolidate any financial troubles you may be having, the lender might call in their loans. This would mean you would have to sell the properties in such a way that would leave you at a loss.

Have a redraw facility or a line of credit

Focusing on the positives is important, but you need to make sure that you are fully prepared for the negatives. Time and time again I see far too few investors heed this advice, and issues end up catching them completely off guard. Many investors don't do enough to ensure that they are protecting their cash flow if times get tough.

By properly setting up a reserve of cash from the very beginning of your career through a line of credit or a redraw facility, you are creating a buffer or cushion for yourself that will give you peace of mind and help you through any financial troubles you may face.

Examine your security regularly

Providing your lenders with too much security is a surefire way to restrict your potential as an investor. Lenders will always tell you that there is no such thing as too much security, but you should review the values of your properties every year. Also, have them re-valued with a bank whenever you notice an increase of around 7%.

Over time, you will be able to remove the security from one of your investment properties, or from your home, granting you more independence and freedom of movement.

Financial considerations

When buying an investment property, there are a couple of things you need to ask yourself regarding your finances, and some issues that you will need to plan for. These will help you decide how you need to plan your finances for future investments.

What return will I get?

In order to be able to calculate your gross yield from a property, you will have to decide what rental you will reasonably be able to charge your tenants. Gross yield is calculated by dividing the annual gross rental by the price you pay for the property. Compare the resulting yield that you will earn with the interest rate that you could get if your money was in the bank.

Keep in mind that holiday homes will not be able to generate a return if you are not willing to rent it out. Also, unless you can keep your holiday home occupied throughout the year, they will only be able to generate an income when they are occupied during the holiday season.

Is my property going to produce a positive cash flow?

We've talked about cash flow in a previous chapter, and how it is imperative to have a profitable property investment career. The ultimate goal when investing in real estate is having your property produce income for you, especially as you draw closer to your retirement. Your primary motivation for purchasing a property should be so that it makes you money, not so much as because it saves you tax.

It is also quite meaningless to acquire great amounts of debt to purchase a property that you think might increase in value. The value of a property might not appreciate the way that you expected it would, or at the rate that you were expecting.

What if interest rates go up or I lose a tenant?

You will need to ensure that you're able to pay the bond and all other expenses like taxes and rates if your tenant moves out and you aren't able to find a new one for a few months. You've got to be able to afford the bond repayments if the bond rates go up by 3 or 4%.

Working this out as soon as you can is vital, as these things can seriously affect your cash flow.

Am I prepared to sell my property if necessary?

An exit strategy is always required for cases where you need to back out of an investment. Unfortunately, there is no time to be sentimental about properties in this industry, and you will have to be fully prepared to sell if the situation becomes dire, and you have to move on.

How many properties can I afford?

It's important to figure out how many properties you will be able to afford based on how you went about financing the acquisition of your first investment property. It's so easy to get swept up with the excitement that comes with buying investment real estate, but you have to consider options only that are affordable and will not put you in any sticky financial situations.

Am I prepared to manage an investment?

As with any investment, property investments need to be managed carefully and properly. You need to think about whether you want to be the sole manager of a property, or whether you want to hire a property manager to take care of it for you. As we've said a few times, property managers are expensive, but they are an excellent investment, especially for those who own a number of properties in different locations. They are great for relieving some of the stress that comes with owning and managing investment properties.

As you can see, there are a lot of things that you need to do to manage your investments properly. Asking the above questions is a vital step that every investor should take before committing their funds to a property, and you should be aware that assessing the performance of your investments on an annual basis is a must.

It's also highly beneficial to educate yourself about the advantages and drawbacks of any kind of investment before you spend any of your money.

Chapter Eight:
Mistakes You Can and Should Avoid

You can't expect to become an expert in real estate investing overnight. Yes, there is good money to be made buying, renting, and selling properties, but doing so takes knowledge, skill, and a lot of determination. While we all know that failure is the best way to learn, it's usually better to learn from other peoples' mistakes rather than make them yourself.

Knowing some of the classic mistakes that other investors make with their properties can help you avoid making them. In this chapter, we are going to discuss some of the most common and often most detrimental mistakes that rookie property investors make, and how you can avoid them.

Failure to plan

You're probably sick of being told that you need to plan, but I cannot stress it enough. The last thing you ever want to do is acquire a property and then figure out what you want to do with it afterward. Resisting the buying frenzy can feel impossible when the market is heated, but it is crucial that you resist the temptation.

Decide on an investment strategy, like one of those that were outlined in *Chapter Three,* before you put in the cash or get a mortgage. Consider the type of property you're looking for. Do you want it to be a vacation destination? A family home? If so, should it be single-family or multi-family? Decide on a plan for purchasing, and then find properties that line up with your plan.

Appreciation-based investments

This is perhaps the most common mistake that investors tend to make. Many people tend to invest in real estate based on the idea that its value will appreciate in the following years. There are a few reasons why this is a terrible idea. Rental property values can and will fluctuate each year, and houses might plummet in value during a down market.

As an investor, you might be required to sell your property unexpectedly, and, when done in a bad market, can cause massive losses. Instead, choose to invest based on a property's cash flow. This is why you need to have a strong idea of the numbers during the investigation process for buying a rental property you intend to keep in your portfolio.

The person that you are buying the property from should be able to give you at least one year's worth of *verifiable* rental numbers *in writing* when you are considering a property to purchase.

Lack of research

Normally, before someone buys a car, they compare different models, ask plenty of questions, and figure out whether it is worth their cash. This same mentality should be applied to purchasing a home but on a far more thorough level. Your research should also be based on the type of investor that you want to be, such as a landlord, a flipper, or a land developer.

In addition to asking a lot of questions regarding the potential property, you should ask about the neighborhood that the property is in as well. Things like nearby commercial or construction sites, known flood zones, replacement fixtures, and crime threats should all be things you inquire about before buying real estate.

Incomplete contracts

When I say 'incomplete', I don't mean contracts that are unfinished, but rather ones that are not comprehensive enough. You should always cover all of your assumptions in the contract when you buy a rental property and be sure to read through them rigorously. When you purchase a property, you're going to have to sign several contracts.

Each of these contracts and real estate partnership agreements need to be read very carefully before you even think of signing them. Missing items can end up costing you a lot of money to fix, and you might even need to contact your lawyer to rectify the problem. It's better to get the contract exactly the way you want it before it's signed, and possibly even hire a lawyer to guide you through this process.

Doing everything alone

A common misconception that buyers tend to have is that they can close a real estate transaction on their own, or that they know it all. Even if you have completed a few deals previously that went well, the process may not be as smooth when the market is down, and there won't be anyone you can call on for help if you want to remedy a property deal that is not ideal.

As a property investor, you should tap into every resource at your disposal, and network with experts that will be able to help you make the best purchases. Your list of potential experts should include people like handymen, home inspectors, real estate agents, and a good attorney. Experts in these fields will be able to fill you in on any flaws that a neighborhood may have.

Inadequate insurance

Insurance is one of the most important aspects of property investments. Having good, comprehensive insurance will help ensure that your investments are protected in case they become damaged from bad weather, like hurricanes or floods. Taking out insurance that isn't tailored to your needs, or not taking out any insurance at all, is another extremely common mistake that investors make.

Choosing the right insurance is just as important as choosing an investment property, and should be carefully considered when buying a rental property. Your insurance policy needs to take into account all of the factors that are specific to your situation, including your financial state and where the property is located.

Overpayment

This is a problem somewhat linked to that of not doing enough research. Finding good real estate to invest in is exhausting, frustrating, and time-consuming. Rookie investors tend to be too hasty to accept the first offer that is made to them when they finally find a property because they do not want to have to keep searching.

The problem with this is that investors will tend to overpay for properties. Doing so can lead to a domino effect of problems in the future. You might end up overextending yourself and accumulating too much debt, which leads to more expensive payments that you won't be able to afford.

The result is a battle to recoup your investment that could last years. If you want to determine whether or not the price tag on a property is too steep, you should find out the prices that other homes in the area have sold for. Real estate brokers can assist you and give you the information that you need without much hassle at all.

Or you could take a look at some of the prices of comparable properties in the local newspaper, or in real estate databases. Unless a home has some unique features that would cause its value to appreciate over time, you should do your best to have your bids be consistent with the other property sales in the area.

Even if you can't reach an agreement with the seller, there will always be other opportunities - something that investors sometimes forget. The chances are that there will be another place out there that is exactly what you're looking for, and for a favorable price as well. Just be patient.

Underestimated expenses

There's a lot more to owning property than merely paying the mortgage, which is something that novice real estate investors tend to forget. There are costs that come with the upkeep of a property and making sure that home appliances like the refrigerator, oven, washer, and dryer are functioning properly. Not to mention the cost of making structural changes to the building.

The best thing to do is to create a list of every monthly expense you will need to pay for maintaining and running the property. In the case of rentals, once you have added the numbers up and you have included the monthly rent, you can calculate the Return On

Investment that will help you figure out if your income will cover the cost of maintenance and mortgage. Below is an example of what such a list should look like:

Mortgage	$22 000
Electricity	$150
Water	$80
Lawn service	$50
Appliances	$500

The values above are fabricated but are there to give you an idea of what your list could contain. Determining these expenses before you purchase a house is essential for house flippers as well since your profits will be tied directly to the time it takes to buy the home, renovate it, and resell it. Regardless, as an investor, developing one of these lists is vital.

You will also need to focus on the short-term costs for financing, cancellation fees, and repayment penalties that might incur when the house is flipped.

Buying too many properties

Like we said in the previous chapter, it's easy to get caught up in a buying frenzy during good markets, especially for first-time investors. It's a good idea to acquire one property so that you can get a feel for the industry. You should also always remember that buying a rental property is a much different experience than buying your first home.

Even if you've already bought your first home, buying a property for the purpose of investment is a totally different process and experience. In nearly all cases, you would be better off buying just one property to start off with. Doing this gives you a good idea of the process and involvement that investing in property requires.

If you can, you should wait at least one year before you purchase any additional properties. This will give you more than enough time to learn and understand everything that owning and managing your own rental property entails. This time frame also lets you work out any issues that you may run into. Think of your first investment property as an opportunity to learn the business of real estate ownership, and to understand it better.

These are all of the main problems that new investors encounter when they enter the industry. Now that you know what they are, and understand what they can cause, avoiding them should be a walk in the park. Be sure to take all of the advice in this chapter into consideration!

Chapter Nine:
Expanding Your Horizons

The logical next step for investors who have made their first investment property purchase is to acquire more properties. Many property investors have portfolios that consist only of one or two properties, because they don't know how to manage a larger portfolio - at least not the right way.

But why do investors avoid buying more than three properties? Well, how many properties do you think you could afford if each of them cost you $1000 a month to own. Unless you are earning more than $200 000 every year, the right answer is 'not a lot.'

You only have so much disposable income to spend on property, and since most investors purchase properties that they have to pay for each month, you quickly deplete your disposable income. So, how are you going to acquire more real estate and expand your portfolio?

That's what we'll be discussing in this chapter.

Leverage your current equity growth

If you already own one or two properties, then you have the ability to speed up your property growth by leveraging the equity that you have in them. Trying to save up your deposits is a very slow and arduous process. If you can use the wealth that your current portfolio has accumulated to acquire more real estate, then you will be able to expand your portfolio at a much faster rate.

For example, if you were to buy a property for $300 000 and assume that its value would appreciate to $400 000, then you would have an effective $100 000 equity in that property. This equity would only be available in two ways: you could either sell the property to receive the cash that is left over ($100 000 minus expenses) or you could borrow money against the equity (generally to a maximum of 80%, which would be $80 000).

Using your equity means that you will not need to put any money from your pockets towards buying more properties. The equity from your current properties is used to pay for the deposit. The more properties you buy, the quicker your equity will increase, which will allow you to acquire more properties.

Generate a positive cash flow

Not being able to afford the repayments for service on a property is one of the main reasons that investors do not purchase more real estate. In other words, they purchase property that costs them money, instead of property that makes them money, meaning that they are limiting themselves with how much property they could afford.

Having each of your properties generate a cash flow that is positive would mean that your investments would pay you to own them. You would receive a payout each month that is more than the sum of your expenses, which you could then use to spend, or better yet, invest, to your heart's delight.

Purchasing properties with a positive cash flow has a domino effect - the more positive cash flow properties you own, the more properties you will be able to afford. You are essentially increasing your total disposable income with each property you acquire by increasing the amount of passive income that you earn. Your disposable income is not being decreased like it would be if you were investing in properties that had negative cash flows.

Without cash flow, you can't afford to own, let alone buy, property.

Be able to assess the market quickly

Every great investor with multiple properties in their portfolio is able to scan the market for good deals in the shortest amount of time possible. You need to keep an eye on the market at all times, but you also need to be able to find those hidden gems that will make you a fortune hastily and with ease.

There are a number of tools online that will help you do this. They allow you to find properties that are geared positively easily and quickly, as well as those that are undervalued, require renovating, or ones from buyers that are willing to negotiate a favorable deal. If you choose not to use one of these tools, then you will need to come up with your own way of scanning the market.

Up the value of your current properties

Increasing the value of your properties and their rental incomes is the best way to increase your cash flow and generate more disposable income that can be put towards buying more real estate. This can be done by doing minor and some major renovations to the properties that are currently in your portfolio. A new carpet and a fresh coat of paint will do wonders for the value of your properties.

Don't avoid purchasing properties that are fixer-uppers. These properties are usually the ones that are sold for the lowest prices. Doing some small renovations to such properties will drastically increase their value, which will subsequently increase the amount of money in your pocket each month.

Adding value will increase the rate at which you are able to buy new properties.

Monitor your portfolio closely

It goes without saying that your properties are not going to take care of themselves unless you hire a property manager. Even then, you will need to keep an eye on them to make sure that everything is running smoothly.

You can think of your real estate like a child - if they are left unmonitored, they will cause damage to themselves and the things around them, especially in the early stages. The same things are true for the properties in your portfolio. You will need to monitor them and guide them to improvement and growth. Merely acquiring property and expecting it to take care of itself is the best way to ensure that you're never able to buy another property again.

Look at the finances of your properties and make sure that they are accurate. Monitor their conditions and talk to real estate agents and home improvement companies about things that you can do to increase their value. Screen your tenants carefully, choose them wisely, and make sure that they are paying their rent on time and doing some basic property maintenance. Also, pay attention to your property manager if you have one - if they aren't doing their job properly, or just suck in general, sack them.

Combine positive cash flow with rapid growth

If all of your properties are experiencing rapid appreciation of value, but are not producing a positive cash flow, then you will find that you will be unable to afford to pay your loans. On the other hand, if all of your properties are producing a positive cash flow, but are not experiencing any capital growth, then you are at risk of having no equity that you can use to invest in new real estate.

Your perfect personal combination of rapid growth and positive cash flow is going to depend on your time frame and risk profile. If your goal is to retire in five years, then you will probably want to avoid a property that is geared negatively and instead opt for the cash flow. But, if you are still young and are looking to expand your portfolio quickly and you are happy in your current job, then you likely won't bother with pulling income from your real estate at this point.

In that case, you will want to balance the number of positive cash flow and rapid growth properties that you purchase. This will allow you to be geared neutrally, meaning you won't be out of money, but can still achieve a desirable growth in equity to speed up the growth of your portfolio.

When it's time, do damage control

Don't flog a dead horse' as the old saying goes. The same idea applies to investments that are not bringing in any money. Too often, property investors will maintain a dead investment because they do not want to admit that they have made a loss or acquired a bad investment. They are also too afraid to lose money, so they continue to hold onto properties even when their value drops. Some even keep real estate for over ten years before it returns to its original value, then claim that they 'haven't lost any money.'

Have an investment strategy

Bet you thought you'd read the word 'plan' for the last time two chapters ago. Nope! Planning will never not be important, even when you are buying your 100th property. Knowing your strategy for investment will allow you to form a list of ideas for things you want from your properties.

This will make the property-buying process much easier. You'll be able to narrow your market from every property out there to only the ones that fit into your investment strategy and suit you the best. You end up wasting far less time, and you will generate income faster, which lets you grow your portfolio quickly as well.

Growing your portfolio is an important step that every new property investor needs to take. It is the key to generating more income, which is the goal for most of us. Following the steps mentioned in this chapter will get you growing your portfolio faster than you could ever have imagined, as long as you remain motivated and determined.

Wrapping Up

We've said it time and time again throughout the course of this book, and we'll say it again: being a property investor is not easy. There is a ton of work involved, and you have to be prepared to take on all of the risks and responsibilities that this industry comes with.

But, if you are determined, motivated, and hardworking, you will be able to achieve your financial goals before you know it - and this book will get you there. Whether you are a novice investor just entering the market, or a real estate professional with hundreds of properties to your name, there is something to be learned from this guide for everyone.

If there's one thing to take away from this book, it's that anyone is capable of making their dreams a reality, regardless of their upbringings or backgrounds. Now get out there and get investing!

Disclaimer

This book contains opinions and ideas of the author and is meant to teach the reader informative and helpful knowledge while due care should be taken by the user in the application of the information provided. The instructions and strategies are possibly not right for every reader and there is no guarantee that they work for everyone. Using this book and implementing the information/recipes therein contained is explicitly your own responsibility and risk. This work with all its contents, does not guarantee correctness, completion, quality or correctness of the provided information. Misinformation or misprints cannot be completely eliminated.

Design: Natalia Design

Picture: Kiian Oksana / www.shutterstock.com

Printed in Great Britain
by Amazon